'Social media has become an invaluable tool in my PR armoury by giving me a direct voice to speak directly to members of the media and the general public. This book is a useful guide to using social media effectively.'
Lord Sugar

'Back in the day, the only way to easily communicate with your public was to use mainstream media and analysts as your mouthpieces. Recent years have brought an explosion of real-time communications channels that organizations use to reach their audience directly with valuable online content: videos, ebooks, white papers, photos, infographics, and more – and then have that information shared in social networks and covered by the media. However, many PR professionals still operate as if their only conduit is mainstream media. *Share This* cuts through the hype of social media to help business owners and public relations professionals make the transition to the new world of real-time communications.'
David Meerman Scott
International bestselling author of *The New Rules of Marketing & PR*, now available in over 25 languages from Bulgarian to Vietnamese

'Social media is PR. And this is a book by PR professionals and experts in social media. If you're a PR professional, get the expertise and insights of the CIPR Social Media panel and impress your friends and clients. Gets a +1 from me. Like.'
Paul Mylrea
Director of Communications, BBC

'This crowd-sourced book on social media is a welcome addition to PR literature, as it brings together a range of insights and world-views of social media and helps the sense-making process on its roles, value creation and appropriate strategies. I hope it will be regularly updated, as this is such a fast-moving field.'
Professor Tom Watson
Professor of Public Relations, Bournemouth University

'Blogs like mine set the news agenda for traditional media, PRs would be daft to ignore a book about how old-school spin is dead and full of advice about how to work better now that social media has rewritten the rules.'
Paul Staines (aka Guido Fawkes)

'This book challenges the minds and expands the horizons of PR and marketing professionals operating in today's digital age, providing excellent insight into how to survive and thrive in it.'
Steve Walker, FCIM
EMEA VP Corporate Communications, Oracle Corporation

'Social media presents significant opportunities to the PR industry, and understanding and embracing these is critical to business success. This book covers and shines light on some of the most important topics in social media today. A must read for anyone in the PR business.'

Andrew Bloch
Vice-Chairman and Founder, Frank PR

'If you want to join a conversation on the convergence of digital and PR, this book is the conversation to go for. A series of essays that shakes up the status quo, questions conventional PR practices, and takes thoughtful positions in a social tone that will challenge, engage and entertain the reader. Get it while it's hot!'

Gerry Brown, FCIM
Lead Digital Analyst, Bloor Research

'*Share This* is a brilliant concept – well conceived, well packaged, well written and a "must read" for any PR professional practicing today. To have such a broad compilation of views on social media – written specifically from a PR perspective – is definitely something our industry has been crying out for.'

Trevor Young (aka PR Warrior)
Edelman Australia

'From corporate communications to brand marketing, social is now at the heart of what we do as PR professionals. This book provides outstanding practical guidance developed by some of our industry's most distinguished practitioners and honed through the very methods that they recommend.'

Marshall Manson
Managing Director, Digital, EMEA, Edelman

'When trying to make sense of the rapidly evolving social media world it makes sense to listen to the wisdom of crowds and *Share This: The Social Media Handbook for PR Professionals* does exactly that, being the result of a collaborative, online process using Google Documents. What makes *Share This* really valuable is the assumption that the PR reader isn't starting from scratch; so those with a working knowledge of social media can use the book to provide practical and trend-led insights and apply them to communication challenges today – and probably tomorrow. As PR realises the power of social media to radically change how brands communicate with their audiences, never has there been a better time to read this book.'

Avril Lee
Partner, CEO London, Ketchum Pleon

SHARE THIS

SHARE THIS

The Social Media Handbook
for PR Professionals

Chartered Institute of
Public Relations (CIPR)

Edited by
Stephen Waddington

A John Wiley & Sons, Ltd., Publication

This edition first published 2012
© 2012 John Wiley & Sons Ltd

Registered office
John Wiley & Sons Ltd, The Atrium, Southern Gate, Chichester, West Sussex, PO19 8SQ, United Kingdom

For details of our global editorial offices, for customer services and for information about how to apply for permission to reuse the copyright material in this book please see our website at www.wiley.com.

Reprinted May 2013

Wiley publishes in a variety of print and electronic formats and by print-on-demand. Some material included with standard print versions of this book may not be included in e-books or in print-on-demand. If this book refers to media such as a CD or DVD that is not included in the version you purchased, you may download this material at http://booksupport.wiley.com. For more information about Wiley products, visit www.wiley.com.

Designations used by companies to distinguish their products are often claimed as trademarks. All brand names and product names used in this book and on its cover are trade names, service marks, trademarks or registered trademarks of their respective owners. The publisher and the book are not associated with any product or vendor mentioned in this book. None of the companies referenced within the book have endorsed the book. This publication is designed to provide accurate and authoritative information in regard to the subject matter covered. It is sold on the understanding that the publisher is not engaged in rendering professional services. If professional advice or other expert assistance is required, the services of a competent professional should be sought.

Library of Congress Cataloging-in-Publication Data

Share this : the social media handbook for PR professionals / Chartered Institute of Public Relations (CIPR) ; edited by Stephen Waddington.
    p. cm.
  Includes index.
  ISBN 978-1-118-40484-3 (cloth)
1. Public relations. 2. Social media. I. Waddington, Stephen. II. Chartered Institute of Public Relations.
  HD59.S45156 2012
  659.20285'4678–dc23

                             2012019131

A catalogue record for this book is available from the British Library.

ISBN 978-1-118-40484-3 (hbk) ISBN 978-1-118-40485-0 (ebk)
ISBN 978-1-118-40486-7 (ebk) ISBN 978-1-118-40487-4 (ebk)

Set in 10/14.5 pt FF Scala by Toppan Best-set Premedia Limited
Printed in Great Britain by TJ International Ltd, Padstow, Cornwall, UK

CONTENTS

LIST OF CONTRIBUTORS

Jane Wilson	Chief Executive, CIPR
Stephen Waddington	Managing Director, Speed Communications
Katy Howell	Managing Director, Immediate Future
Simon Sanders	Marketing Consultant
Andrew Smith	Managing Director, Escherman
Helen Nowicka	Head of Digital, UK, Porter Novelli
Gemma Griffiths	Managing Director, The Crowd &I
Becky McMichael	Head of Strategy and Innovation, Ruder Finn
Robin Wilson	Director Digital PR and Social Media, McCann Erickson
Alex Lacey	Senior Corporate Comms Manager, Herbalife Europe
Matt Appleby	Managing Director, Golley Slater PR
Dan Tyte	Director, Working Word Public Relations
Stuart Bruce	Corporate Communications Consultant
Rob Brown	Managing Director, Staniforth
Russell Goldsmith	Digital & Social Media Director at markettiers4dc
Adam Parker	Chief Executive, Realwire
Julio Romo	Communications Consultant
Philip Sheldrake	Founding Partner, Meanwhile
Richard Bagnall	Board Director of Gorkana Group, MD of Metrica
Daljit Bhurji	Managing Director, Diffusion
Richard Bailey	Senior Lecturer in Public Relations, Leeds Metropolitan University
Rachel Miller	Senior Internal Communications Manager
Mark Pack	Head of Digital, MHP Communications
Simon Collister	Senior Lecturer at University of the Arts London

FOREWORD

Jane Wilson CEO, CIPR

The media through which humans communicate are constantly evolving, reflecting changes in technology and preferences in content and consumption. In public relations, communicating messages through a variety of media is the primary means by which we engage audiences in dialogue to develop mutual understanding and deliver against organisational objectives. As the media we use change, so must the practice of public relations.

Currently, a rapid evolution in media is taking place. Through the choices, made by millions every second of each day, to share and curate content, individuals the world over are engaging with each other on a scale unimaginable to most people just a decade ago.

Previous modes of media allowed for the transmission of information, filling a human desire for knowledge, but could not cater for the human impulse to interact. This is changing not only our profession, but society for the better.

For thirty years or more public relations was a mostly misapplied term, synonymous with the transmission of messages through news media. The practice of public relations focused on the management of relations with the gatekeepers to these media to the point where popular culture typically reflects a misunderstanding of our profession, labelled 'PR'.

The evolution of media offers us an opportunity to take public relations back to a better understanding of itself. By providing us with the ability to listen to our audience, to reach them individually and as groups and with a new depth of data available to help us measure the outcome of this activity, and all in real time, we can achieve genuine dialogue by encouraging and participating in conversations. Social media may help public relations realise its potential contribution to the achievement of strategic objectives in an even more meaningful way.

To maximise this opportunity we need to adapt our skills to the media through which we seek to engage. This book is not a starting point. It assumes the reader has a better than basic understanding and is looking to move even farther ahead with expert guidance. It discusses how the evolution of media is changing areas of professional practice such as public affairs and internal communications. It looks at public and private sector public relations. It reminds us that, as paid advocates, we should tread carefully. We do not own the media space, our audiences do.

I am grateful to the experts, drawn from both members and non-members, who have shaped this book with their contributions and are actively shaping our profession with their willingness to share their knowledge. The Institute is particularly indebted to Stephen Waddington, who coordinated the authors and did more than any other person to bring it about. Sharing is the essence of our current media age. Learn from this handbook and share your experiences with us on the CIPR Conversation.[1]

---

[1] CIPR Conversation: http://cipr.co/cipr-conversation

INTRODUCTION

Stephen Waddington, Editor

In time we'll come to stop using the term social media as a catch-all phrase to describe the creation and sharing of content and it will become the norm. *Share This: The Social Media Handbook for PR Professionals* has been written to help accelerate that timescale.

In 2012 all media must be social – and public relations practitioners who want to continue to work in the industry must quickly adapt to this new environment.

The book developed out of a series of Summer Social workshops run by the CIPR's Social Media Panel during the summers of 2010 and 2011 by Philip Sheldrake and Gemma Griffiths. Each week, people turned up to events around the country to hear experts – many of whom feature in this book – lead conversations about different aspects of the development of public relations.

At the end of the summer of 2011, the CIPR's Social Media Panel decided to record and replay some of the conversations from these sessions in a book to share with practitioners more widely.

Share This is itself a social effort. We've pushed the boundaries of book production, which, in itself, has been an interesting process.

The book was conceived and written over a three-month period by 24 public relations practitioners representing a cross-section of public, private and voluntary sector expertise. The project was managed via a series of Google Documents with contributors reviewing and commenting on each other's work.

Each chapter has been written as a standalone piece of work and is intended to be read independently. You can either choose the topics that interest you or read the entire book from start to finish.

My thanks to everyone who volunteered their time to contribute to the project and tolerated my persistent hounding against deadlines. Special thanks are due to Philip Sheldrake for his drive and support. Finally, thanks to Phil Morgan, Andrew Ross, and the team at the CIPR for recognising the potential of this project and supporting us in bringing it to fruition.

Part I

Changing Media, Changing PR

Chapter 1

Katy Howell

The meteoric rise of social network sites like Facebook, Twitter and YouTube changed the communications landscape forever. But social media are vastly more diverse: a connected and complex ecosystem founded on relationships, passions and a desire to be connected.

Social networks are not new. As individuals, we have always maintained social connections, be they with family, friends or professional acquaintances. We belong to groups, clubs, neighbourhoods and, of course, society. The internet and developments in technology have simply made our networks visible and easily accessible. We can now meet friends and colleagues, ask for recommendations and even build relationships with brands – in an online and often public space.

It's big, it's connected and it's here to stay

More than 70% of the internet population uses social networks in one form or another[2] and the numbers are growing daily. One in nine people[3] on Earth have a Facebook account, and if it was a country, it would be the third largest

---

[2] ETC New Media Trend Watch, Social Media and UGC: http://cipr.co/zvoJKl

[3] This number is calculated by dividing the planet's 6.94 billion people by Facebook's 750 million users.

after China and India. Even relative newcomer Instagram has gathered 12 million members[4] in less than a year.

And whilst the landscape continues to grow and change apace, our audiences have moved beyond the media hype and embraced new communication channels wholeheartedly. Social networking already accounts for 1 in every 6 minutes spent online.[5]

Being social online isn't restricted to 'Generation Y'. At the time of writing, the average profile age on Twitter is 35 years, and a bit older on LinkedIn, at 40. Facebook's biggest demographic is now between 35 and 54 years. Even YouTube has an even spread of users right across the 20–55 age range.

But, more significant than just the volume and demographics of participants is the change in the way people communicate, and changes in the way people are connecting, collaborating and building relationships online. A change in the way people are demanding, sharing and creating content. From user-generated content to link sharing, the frequency of participation in social networks is intense.

When it comes to sharing, the volume of content circulating through the networks is staggering. Every minute, 60 hours of video is uploaded to YouTube, 3000 images go up on Flickr and more than 700 YouTube links[6] are Tweeted. Conversations, too, demonstrate the enthusiasm for connecting online. There are 95 million Tweets a day, 85% of bloggers post more than once a week,[7] and 57% of people talk more online than they do in real life.[8]

The rich and complex picture of social media is still evolving. As the networks grow and the conversations proliferate, people are increasingly engaged. Add mobile to the mix and you now have always-online, connected everywhere, through any device, social networkers.

---

[4]TechCrunch, Instagram Now Has 12 Million Users, 100K Weekly Downloads In China Alone, Alexia Tsotsis, 31 October 2011: http://cipr.co/AyWOMj

[5]comScore, The Network Effect: Facebook, LinkedIn, Twitter and Tumblr reach new heights in May, Andrew Lipsman, 15 June 2011: http://cipr.co/wzE8pW

[6]YouTube Statistics, as of 8 March 2012: http://cipr.co/x9pYW8

[7]SlideShare, Technorati Blogging Stats Preview, Eric Schwarztman: http://cipr.co/woDkZo

[8]Source Alex Trimpe via Ogilvy – 21 February 2011, ThinkQuarterly, Google.

And even when the statistics in this chapter need revising (probably in a matter of weeks), it is clear that social networks are part of our lives and they are here to stay.

People connect, technology facilitates

In truth, no matter the demographic, device or even the numbers, human beings are motivated to connect and share for a multitude of reasons:[9] researching, finding information and inspiration, participating, connecting with friends and for entertainment. Social network sites are the vehicle, not the destination.

Although 'to Facebook' appears to have entered the vernacular as a common verb, it is not social networking platforms that drive the conversation – it is people. People connect to share interests, passions and friendships, with content as the catalyst for conversations. This is demonstrated when conversations around topics are mapped online. It becomes clear that both people and conversations will move across the different social platforms. Migrating and coalescing in different online locations.

The BBC's weekly political debate programme, *Question Time*, is a good example of how interest and conversation will move across the different types of social network. In between broadcasts the programme's current topics of the week are debated in forums, on blogs and within the BBC website itself. But as the programme goes live, the conversation jumps to Twitter, with a rapid stream of 140-character opinions attached to the hashtag, #bbcqt. As the broadcast finishes, the conversation slides back to longer debates on other social networks.

The result is that connection and communities are spread across the social landscape in a fire hose of conversations. With so much chatter, it becomes difficult to find and join conversations or to network. But, it is again technology that can help people navigate the social landscape. Most social networks

---

[9]Jeffesposito.com, 15 interesting facts about social media in the UK, Adam Vincenzini, 16 February 2011: http://cipr.co/w9AKZZ

are designed with functionality to help users find connections and topics of interest within them. However, it is still a challenge to find relevant conversations and communities across the whole social landscape.

The search engines recognise that people want to source information from their trusted networks. They also understand the value of human filtering to identify valued content. Both Google and Microsoft Bing are incorporating social conversations (and social signals) into their results.

And whilst the algorithms used to rank content are still very much a secret, it seems that 'Likes' on Facebook or Google's +1 recommendation and social referrals are impacting the ranking of information. Now when people search, their own social network (called the social graph) impacts results. This is called 'social search'. It narrows the results for the searcher, making visible content created or touched by users within their social graph.

It isn't just in searching for relevant content and conversations that technology facilitates social networking. It is technology, too, that empowers our online voice. Technology provides social network platforms that are easy to use, facilitate sharing and make it simple to connect to our friends, peers and/ or any company we choose.

Explaining the plethora of social network sites

Whenever social media are mentioned, it seems that Facebook and Twitter dominate the discussion. After all, it is these well-known social networks that the traditional media consistently reference. The adverts and programmes we watch entice us to like Fan Pages and use Twitter hashtags, whilst the tabloids flash us headlines on the evils of social networks (while encouraging us to 'share' the very same stories with our own social network!) They are now part of the mainstream.

Of course the social media landscape is far more complex. It is an ecosystem of differing styles and types of network: networks and platforms that range from self-publishing and content sharing, through to discussion boards and virtual worlds. What they have in common, though, are principles founded on Web 2.0 technology.[10] Principles that ensure communications are two-way, interactive and, above all, shareable.

Although they have a common foundation in technology, social networks don't fit quite so neatly into categories or types. Constantly evolving to become more useful to their users, we see new applications and services launch, such as group buying and smartphone photo sharing. Established social networks, too, absorb new functionality. You are just as likely to view a video embedded on Facebook or Tumblr as you are to see it on YouTube.

Putting the complexity of creating a detailed classification aside, there is value in identifying the main types of social media platform. Understanding the primary rationale for the different social networks is invaluable when evaluating where, how and when to communicate.

Networking sites

Networking sites should not be confused with the term 'social networks'. The latter is an umbrella phrase that encompasses all the differing types of social media, platforms and connections.

A networking site is an online service made up of individuals and is most recognisable by the user profiles. Networkers connect with links to friends, sharing common interests, passions, ideas and content. Ultimately they are designed to enable people to socialise online.

Facebook is the most recognisable site. It was originally created for students and now accounts for 58% of all visits to social sites.[11] But there are many more networking sites, including the relative newcomer Google+, and there is significant variation in popularity from one country to the next.

Then there are networking sites that have a specific focus. The best example is LinkedIn, which is a business-related site and is mainly used for professional networking.

Some networks are popular in certain countries. Hyves is popular in the Netherlands, StudiVZ in Germany, Tuenti in Spain, Nasza-Klasa in Poland

---

[10] O'Reilly Media, What Is Web 2.0: http://cipr.co/wYoQza
[11] Data from Experian Hitwise white paper, 'Carpe Diem – Seizing the moment in social media': http://cipr.co/yePdFC

and Skyrock in various parts of Europe. But it is Orkut and Hi5 that lead the conversations in South America and Mixi and Cyworld in Asia.

Blogs

In February 2011 there were estimated to be more than 156 million public blogs in existence.[12] Created in a diary style format, they represent the opinions and thoughts of the writer. Technology platforms such as WordPress, Blogger and TypePad can also be used to create forums, news feeds and even websites.

Influential and connected blogs are frequently updated and have lots of comments. Subject matter and interests vary across a vast spectrum of topics. There are news blogs, like The Huffington Post; passion-led blogs, such as Maison Cupcake Blog; and leading industry blogs, such as Mashable and TechCrunch.

Microblogs

Microblogging is a short form of blogging – typically no more than 140–200 characters per post. The most recognisable platform is Twitter, although Tumblr is quickly grabbing the public's attention (it receives the second highest number of page views from any social media platform after Facebook[13]). Other platforms include FriendFeed, Posterous and the microblog for private use within organisations, Yammer.

Collaborative communities

Some social networks see users collaborate to achieve a single goal. The oldest and most recognised collaborative site is Wikipedia. But it isn't the only wiki. There are numerous wiki platforms[14] and a wide variety of sites covering

---

[12]State of the Media: The Social Media Report Q3 2011, NMIncite, Nielsen: http://cipr.co/xUs9EN
[13]Ibid. 12
[14]Wikipedia, Comparison of wiki software: http://cipr.co/wwWJgs

issues from medicine to wine tasting, and, of course, the CIPR social media wiki.[15]

Sites that facilitate collaborative buying (or group buying to get a better deal) also proliferate. Most well known are Groupon and LivingSocial. But it isn't just discounts that are driving collaborative purchasing. So, too, is the rise of collaborative consumption.[16] Whether it's car sharing with Streetcar or hiring a room with Crashpadder, social media are facilitating the cultural shift towards sharing possessions.

Communities and forums

Communities and forums proliferate across the Web; some launching and disappearing almost overnight and others becoming as established as the mainstream media. There is no one typical approach to them. So below are a few of the most prevalent types of forum.

Discussion-based forums tend to create close-knit and trusted communities. Often based around specific interests and driven by a passionate and vocal membership, the range of conversations can be quite broad. Take a look at Mumsnet.com or Moneysavingexpert.com, where discussions focus on parenting and finances respectively. These communities can be deceptively large (Mumsnet has more than 1.5 million monthly unique users[17]).

Review communities have blossomed to help people identify great services and products and avoid those that have disappointed others. In fact, a recent survey shows that 42% of people have written a product review online.[18] These communities focus on reviews, usually on specific topics. Probably the best known are TripAdvisor and Review Centre, but there are specialist sites such as 'White Goods Help' and the entertainment site Metacritic.

Some businesses that want to create their own networks have launched *branded communities*. Not all have been successful, but some have tapped into interests to create strong, interactive experiences for their audiences.

---

[15]CIPR Social Media Panel wiki: http://cipr.co/ciprsm-wiki
[16]Collaborative Consumption Hub: http://cipr.co/xGrrhN
[17]Statistic from Mumsnet Google Analytics: http://cipr.co/ypFamK
[18]SlideShare, The Science of Sharing: An inside look at a consumer: http://cipr.co/wkwMgu

Mothercare launched the successful Gurgle.com for parents (now in the US and India too); BT Tradespaces is thriving with its membership of small businesses; and some communities, such as Weightwatchers, are extensions of the brand website.

Finally, there are *DIY communities*. Here, individuals or groups create their own social network using services such as Ning or BuddyPress. Alternatively, communities are founded within established social networks such as Facebook Pages or LinkedIn Groups.

Content-sharing communities

With the profusion of social networks and subsequent conversations has come a deluge of content. From videos and pictures to links and music, it seems content can be found everywhere. And not just content published by companies, but user-generated content. Much of this content is stored and found on social networks that focus on sharing, ranking and sorting.

Photo sharing is exemplified by Flickr – a site with more than 51 million registered users.[19] Here, users can publish photos, share and even sell them. Other photo-sharing networks include Zoomr and Photobucket and photo apps such as Instagram.

Video sharing is an established cornerstone of social networking, accounting for over 4% of all internet usage. YouTube is the most popular, accounting for nearly 70% of all visits to video websites.[20] Other platforms include Vimeo, Dailymotion, Redux and Metacafe.

The internet has revolutionised the way in which fans listen to music. But it is social networks that have allowed people to share their preferences and current listening habits, often in real time. Spotify, SoundCloud, Last.FM, Gogoyoko and Playlist are just a handful of the music-sharing platforms. Even the ubiquitous iTunes has Ping – where users can follow their favourite artists and friends to discover what music they are talking about, listening to and downloading.

---

[19]Yahoo!, About Flickr: http://cipr.co/xggElr
[20]Statistic from Experian Hitwise white paper, 'Online Video: Bringing Social Media To Life': http://cipr.co/AoHYRt

Bookmarking is the simplest and easiest form of content sharing. Bookmarking sites such as StumbleUpon, Digg, Pinboard and Reddit, allow users to organise links, tag, add notes or comments and then share them. Some sites, such as Digg, encourage voting to rank the links; others, like Delicious, help you to organise your links into 'stacks' around content themes.

Geo-social networks

Whilst some social networks, such as Twitter and Facebook, allow user location to be added to posts using geolocation, there are also specific geo-social networks such as Gowalla and Foursquare. Geolocation allows users to tag current locations, create a comment about the place or 'check in'. Adoption of these services is still quite small. However, as more people connect to social networks via mobile, it is likely that the use of geolocation services will continue to grow.

Virtual worlds

One of the most recognised virtual worlds is Second Life, unless you are an RPG gamer, in which case you will be familiar with World of Warcraft and its 10-million-strong user base. Virtual worlds are online communities within computer-simulated environments, where users interact with one another through avatars. There is still little mass adoption of these technologies and very few demographic or usage data. But it is a network to keep on your radar for the future.

PRs need to understand the social network landscape

For today's PR practitioner, adapting public relations to this changing environment can seem daunting. Social networks present a complex, but rich, landscape of opportunities and risks.

The focus must always be on the communities, whether they are connected through interest groups, trusted friendships or driven by passions.

Tapping into the conversations that are relevant to your stakeholders allows businesses to build relationships, influence communications and ultimately inspire advocacy and trust.

Katy Howell (@katyhowell) is the managing director of one of the most respected social media consultancies, immediate future. She helps companies navigate the social media landscape – working closely with businesses to develop social business plans and training, set out frameworks, recommend strategies and design communication blueprints. She creates robust, measurable initiatives, whilst managing the risk to reputation.

Part II

Planning

Chapter 2

KICK-START YOUR SOCIAL MEDIA STRATEGY

Simon Sanders

Many organisations now use social media. But not all do so strategically, and some don't use social media at all. The six steps outlined here aim to help you overcome any obstacles or inertia and kick-start your social media strategy.

Is your organisation currently using social media? Millions of organisations around the world are publishing their latest news and engaging via Twitter, Facebook or a company blog, perhaps even uploading videos to YouTube, maintaining a company profile on LinkedIn and exploring the possibilities of Google+. For many it's a journey of discovery as they look to find new ways to engage with customers and other stakeholders. Not everyone is at it though: Econsultancy's State of Social Media Report 2011[21] surveyed more than 1000 clients, brands, marketing, digital and PR agencies and noted that around 35% are either still at a very experimental stage or not doing any social media activity at all.

1. Select your squad

In time it will impact every part of an organisation – yet in some businesses social media are not so much seen as a wonderful opportunity but as a worrying threat, and in others just an irrelevant distraction. To date it has tended to be the PR, marketing and customer services functions that have been at

---

[21]Econsultancy's State of Social Media Report 2011: http://cipr.co/zkpIuu

the forefront of using social media. Yet there are plenty of commonplace situations which show how different areas of a business might well have to be involved, as the following scenarios illustrate (with sample suggestions of business areas involved shown in brackets):

- Customers complaining about urgent problems with products (customer services; PR).
- Workers mocking their employers or the company's customers (corp. comms; HR).
- Negative/slanderous content that has been published and shared (legal; PR).
- Constructive suggestions about how a company could do things better (R&D; insight).
- Competitors promoting offers directly and making direct sales (sales; marketing).

As you can see, being active in social media might require input from and collaboration with many other parts of the business. In a large organisation, this could involve multiple stakeholders, whereas in a smaller organisation, these roles might all be covered by a handful of people. The overarching point is that to overcome any inertia and rise to the opportunities and threats, you will probably need to take a few people with you on your journey – keeping them up to date with your plans and actions, and getting their input along the way. As well as getting the buy-in you need now, you may be able to build the support you may rely on later. As a side note: if you are going to be leading the introduction and integration of social media into your organisation, it will be worth reading Jeremiah Owyang's insights into alternate frameworks for your social media structure.[22]

2. Choose a goal

Remember Lewis Carroll's Cheshire Cat from *Alice's Adventures in Wonderland*? It noted 'if you don't know where you are going, any road will get you

---

[22]Jeremiah Owyang on alternate frameworks for social media structures: http://cipr.co/AdX6Xe

there.' Such is the way with social media. So, before you rush to establish a social media presence without a clear purpose, you must first consider what the point of your social media activity is. What would you like to achieve?

To help kick-start your strategy, consider the following three business drivers and associated PR goals that social media can address.

Business Driver	Social Media Goal	Achieving What?
Brand	Awareness	Earning attention/reaching more people/ building profile
Finance	Sales	Generating enquiries, leads or sales
Customers	Loyalty	Keeping stakeholders engaged/ maintaining reputation/encouraging repeat business

For PR people, Awareness and Loyalty probably chime the loudest as the most natural fit but, ask yourself, for you and your organisation, does any one of these three goals leap off the page as the single most important? You may want to select them all but, to kick-start your social media manoeuvres, you might wish to choose just one to prioritise and focus on. Pick more than one if you wish, but recognise that it will probably mean a separate strategy for each goal, and more resources to achieve them.

Whatever you decide, whichever you choose, the ideal situation is to firmly align your social media goals with the core drivers of your organisation's success. In this way, your social media achievements are most likely to be judged – and hopefully as successful – at the most senior levels.

3. Start listening

As *The Cluetrain Manifesto*[23] pointed out, every market is a conversation – and your own marketplace is likely to be full of conversations, content and communities to tune into. A social media listening exercise will focus on your entire online environment: not just what is being said about you, but your

---

[23] *The Cluetrain Manifesto*: http://cipr.co/w6oILi

wider product or service 'keywords', your senior people, colleagues or employees, your competitors, your industry sector and your wider stakeholder environment. It should – or at least could – uncover all sorts of interesting results, allowing you to discover what others are talking about before you join the conversation.

You might discover comments and observations on Twitter or Facebook, detailed opinions on review sites or queries and answers posted in forums. You might discover relevant bloggers writing about your sector, how competitors or challengers are embracing social media and content from fellow colleagues, suppliers or partners. Against this backdrop, it's not hard to see why pushing out one-way messages, replicating the advertising or press-release model of communications, fails to embrace the potential to engage with people in social media.

There is a range of listening tools you can use to discover what and where the conversation is. Some, like Google Alerts or Social Mention, are free and will email you when they discover new mentions of your chosen keywords. Others, like TweetDeck and HootSuite, provide an online dashboard with which you can monitor multiple keywords in channels such as Twitter, but also use it to post your own content and links or reply to other users. More advanced platforms, including the likes of Radian6, Sysomos, SM2 and Brandwatch, are available on a paid-for subscription basis: they let you monitor, analyse and drill down into the data to identify the key media, channels, influencers and sentiment and to assign tasks to others in your team to ensure the right response. Tools like these equip you not just to listen but also to participate.

4. Think character and content

Social media are about presenting the human side of your business, engaging with your audience to build trust, understanding and brand loyalty. As Tony Hsieh, CEO of Zappos, one of the biggest social media success stories, noted, 'people relate to people, not companies.' Being human is natural to (most) humans but how does an organisation do it?

Consider the difference between image and character. Image is about the 'for show' veneer we might use to portray ourselves or else might judge others by from afar. By contrast, character is about the 'real' person that we or others get to know from a more close-at-hand perspective. For your organisation, then, becoming more human might be about reducing the distance between you and your audience – perhaps showing yourself to be open, reliable, responsive, friendly or engaging. These character traits could be very different to how your organisation talks in other, more formal marketing communications which are more reliant on image – and this more human side need not mean you can't still be inspiring or authoritative.

In practical terms, then, you might reveal your human side through customer service teams responding to queries on Twitter; through blog or video posts featuring your CEO or other people in the business that people might like to hear from; through relationship building with potential influencers or bloggers. Of course, the focus needn't solely be on your people: you could choose to feature your audience. How could collecting and reflecting stories about how your customers are using your products help humanise you? Could telling their story, help you tell your story? Would using their actual words or voices, showing their faces, places or spaces help you create deeper, more memorable or meaningful content which could help earn you attention, create an affinity, drive loyalty or attract new customers?

Within your overall strategy you will need to plan out a content strategy. This will map out the mix of different types of content you should be creating and sharing with your audience, and a schedule for the months, weeks and individual days. It will pay to bear in mind the 'Technographics' studies from Forrester Research[24] or the 9Cs of Social Media User Types[25] research by this author for Lansons Communications, which built on this by understanding whether your audience is, for example, likely to comprise creators of content or, say, simply critics, conversationalists or just passive consumers; knowing this, you can better judge the type of content that will produce the best engagement.

---

[24]'Technographics' work by Forrester Research: http://cipr.co/zLmtsn
[25]Lansons Communications, UK Social Media Census 2011: http://cipr.co/z5HSot

5. Integrate your outposts

With social media strategy, the platforms you choose to use should be decided last. The big four are Facebook, Twitter, YouTube and LinkedIn, but it really will depend on you, your audience and how they use social media. Whichever you use, the way to think about these platforms is as outposts or embassies that support your main website.

The aim is two-fold: firstly, you want to direct traffic from the inside >> outward so that casual visitors to your website can opt to stay connected to you through one of your social media outposts. In this way, they might continue to hear from you and consume your content without having had to deliberately visit your website again. Secondly, you will want to direct traffic from the outside >> inward so that those engaging with your content at your outposts might be tempted to visit the website. In this way, you can deliver users right to the specific landing pages on your website where they can 'convert' or perform some other desirable action.

Of course, the potential of social media is that as well as being in contact with your immediate audience, you can also reach others via the 'Likes', '+1s', comments, favourites and so on, that act as votes and recommendations for your content. By creating content that engages people, they will actively or passively share it with their network.

You should also look to integrate social media with other channel activity, such as your email, and even offline events where you can still capture new fans and followers. Further technical integration should also be sought, in particular with your Web Analytics and if possible your CRM (Customer Relationship Management) system. These steps will really help you track and prove your success.

6. Measure what you treasure

Whatever your strategy, you need to know if you are getting results. Much of the talk in social media, digital and PR circles has been about the ROI (return on investment) that social media can offer. To sum up the story so far, critics query investment in social media without any clear metrics for success.

Advocates of social media point out that the ROI of other marketing activities (e.g. TV advertising) is no more clear-cut and that other aspects of PR aren't always held to such direct account (e.g. how did a mention in a magazine article translate to more retail sales?)

A great deal of heat and light has been expended on potential metrics or KPIs (key performance indicators) that could be used to measure success. A list created by Chris Lake for Econsultancy[26] considers more than 30 different micro-measures such as number of new fans or followers, comments to a blog, views of a video and so on.

It is worth remembering a quote attributed to Einstein, namely that 'not everything that can be counted counts, and not everything that counts can be counted'. The most important thing to focus on will be simply whatever shows you have achieved your goal(s).

If Awareness was the key goal, you might look to show increased brand mentions in social media. You might show how you have earned a greater share of online voice or positive recommendations in your niche. Using external services like Google Insights for Search,[27] you might detect an increase in searches for your brand keywords.

Where your goal is Sales focused, your website traffic data (e.g. via Google Analytics[28]) might help you attribute a rise in visits, page views and conversions to links shared in social media. You might even be able to show how you have achieved a reduction in paid search costs (e.g. via Google AdWords[29]) as a result of more direct visits to your site without the need to buy traffic via keyword bidding. There also remains the potential for F-commerce solutions whereby brands transact with customers from within Facebook. This has already been done by, for example, ASOS clothing and again offers up potential as something to be measured.

For Loyalty goals connected with reputation and retention, success could be measured by looking at, say, a reduction in complaints in social media or

---

[26]Econsultancy, Chris Lake, Are you measuring the right social media metrics?: http://cipr.co/wDSXA2
[27]Google Insights for Search: http://cipr.co/wSMbUL
[28]Google Analytics: http://cipr.co/ypv3zz
[29]Google AdWords: http://cipr.co/yj4RBk

perhaps an increase in completed customer service queries. Other considerations could be increased advocacy on forums or blogs or increased reach or engagement with Twitter users or on Facebook.

Kick-start. Full stop

This chapter has reached its end, but I hope it provides a useful starting point for your own social media adventures. It may have only provided a taste of some of the necessary considerations, but the intention is that you might adopt or adapt the framework to your own needs and duly kick-start your own social media strategy.

Simon Sanders (@simonsanders) has 20 years of marketing, advertising and PR experience gained in agencies, client-side and with media owners, working across consumer, financial, corporate and government sectors. His roles include writing and producing commercials; planning and buying media; creating sponsored programming and brand partnerships; and developing digital PR and social media programmes.

Chapter 3

Andrew Smith

Google launched in September 1998. In the space of 14 years, Google's search engine has become as familiar (and possibly as indispensable) as breathing. Imagine if it disappeared tomorrow. We'd be lost. What has Google done for PR in that time?

What has Google done for PR? A flippant answer: a lot.

A better way to look at this is to first ask: what has Google done *to* the PR industry?

On a very mundane level, Google has given PRs a cheap way of monitoring online brand mentions (Google Alerts) as well as a real-time news monitor (Google News).

On a more indirect level, Google has given rise to a whole new industry devoted to Search Engine Optimisation (SEO) and Pay-Per-Click (PPC) advertising – both areas that take growing amounts of an ever-shrinking marketing-budget pie. Indeed, SEO is talked of by some as 'PR's lost opportunity.' However, that suggests that PR had an opportunity to grasp in the first place. I'm not sure it did (but it certainly has one now).

SEO rose largely on the back of a technical understanding of how Google's search algorithm actually worked. The early years of SEO were characterised by focusing on the 'on page' elements of search optimisation – such as making sure keywords were contained in title tags, creating site maps and so forth. The PPC brigade also brought with it some techniques from the land of direct marketing. Namely, the concept of testing and a laser focus on conversion metrics. There was also not inconsiderable effort spent building robust analytical processes.

And where was PR when all this was going on? Largely still doing pretty much what it has done for the last several decades – albeit with a thin digital veneer laid on top. PR, on the whole, still focuses on 'pitching to the media'. We may try dressing it up by talk of creating 'compelling content' and 'engaging with audiences'. But if we are honest, much of traditional PR is still tied to the mast of journalism – a ship that, if not sinking completely, is certainly sailing through its own stormy waters.

In terms of measurement, PR has generally relied upon vanity metrics such as Advertising Value Equivalence, Reach and Opportunities To See. Digital marketers often shake their heads at this. It is the equivalent of saying 'I gained 1 million impressions. But I didn't get anyone to click on the ad.' Or at least, I have no way of knowing what they did as a result of being exposed to my content (although this is an accountability problem shared by advertising and other elements of the traditional marketing mix).

In the parallel world of digital marketing, practitioners have been able to use data to better understand real audience behaviour and to test what things really do have a measurable impact on real business objectives.

But before we leave the room of PR and turn out the light, I'd suggest all is not lost – quite the reverse. However, PR practitioners are going to have to put some effort into taking a more robust attitude to using data to better understand audience behaviour and measuring outcomes.

To begin answering our original question, Google has made us rethink how reputation is filtered in the age of digital.

Google Search has been described as both a reputation engine and a database of intentions. It is both of these things – and more.

You only have to consider your own experience. If you checked your own browser history you would probably surprise yourself at the number of search queries you make in a typical day. Current estimates suggest there are 34,000 Google Search queries carried out every second of every day around the world. Each one of those searches has behind it some kind of intent or motivation. The individual may be looking for information. They may be using Google navigationally (rather than bookmark a page, you simply type in a keyword to get the URL you want – which explains why terms like Google and Facebook still figure in the top ten of most popular search terms). They may be looking to buy something. They may be seeking out multimedia content (e.g. YouTube).

The search results returned when people use Google have a major impact on how they behave and interact with a brand or organisation. The coveted number one position in Google's Search Results Pages bestows on the recipient the lion's share of traffic related to the query of the searcher. Given that the vast majority of click throughs will end up going via a natural search result rather than a PPC ad, it is easy to see why attempts to gain that number one slot are so highly prized.

But what role has PR played in this process to date? There is a vague notion that good online press coverage helps in some way (but with no hard data or analysis to back this up). Perhaps worse, as Kelvin Newman of leading SEO firm SiteVisibility says, 'We all understand that Google's algorithm is trying to mimic the real world. Google's reliance on links to determine authority is based on what happens offline. If a trusted person or media outlet recommends a product, the more I trust the recommendation. And the more likely I am to believe them. Makes sense, doesn't it? So why do so many people believe that Press Release Syndication services (who will shill for anyone who hands over the cash) are going to be good for your rankings? Huge swathes of the PR industry think that in order to 'get' SEO they just have to start adding a few keywords into their press releases, bung them on a wire and their clients will automatically shoot up the rankings.'

The fact is that PR can and should have a much more involved role in helping organisations best understand the online reputation landscape they are operating in – and what techniques and activities are more likely to succeed than not. However, without a more robust understanding of how Google works (and the tools available), PR is likely to continue to lose out to established SEO firms.

One of the key things Google has brought to the PR party is some of the most useful audience behaviour data imaginable. Take the use of Google's Insights tool. Within a matter of minutes, it is possible to get insight into the levels of interest in particular keyword terms and phrases (and, by definition, relative levels of desire, intent and behaviour). Not only this, but if Google has a significant amount of historical data for the term, then it can provide a prediction as to likely search volume in the future. It doesn't take much to extrapolate to see how this could be hugely useful from a planning perspective. If you know, for example, that interest is likely to peak at certain times of the year, you may choose to focus your PR efforts around these times.

The fact that the Bank of England recently published a white paper outlining how it is using Google Insights to gain more timely and accurate insight into a range of economic indicators shows just how powerful a tool this really is. It would seem foolish for the PR industry not to make full use of such a tool to help plan and shape more effective communications activities.

We should bear in mind that this is but one of a number of tools provided by Google. If PR professionals were better informed as to how to use them, it could help PR provide a far more robust justification of its value.

But we still have some way to go.

In March 2010, I gave a presentation on PR and SEO at the CIPR HQ in Russell Square, London, to around 75 senior in-house communications directors and managers. I asked how many of them used Google Analytics[30] data from their own corporate sites to inform their PR and communications strategies. Not a single hand went up.

In a similar vein, there was little awareness (let alone use) of free Google tools such as Insights, Ad Planner and the Keyword Tool. These tools are freely available. With a little effort and imagination, they can help to transform our whole approach to PR message development, content creation and campaign planning.

Let's look at some of these tools and concepts in turn to see how they might be applied in a traditional PR context.

Google Analytics

Here are some quick wins for PRs using Google Analytics data:

- Bounce rate (or, as Google Analytics Evangelist Avinash Kaushik so memorably described it – they came, they puked, they left[31]). If a client website

---

[30]Google Analytics: http://cipr.co/ypv3zz
[31]Avinash Kaushik, Occam's Razor: http://cipr.co/zhO4oj

has a high bounce rate, i.e. 75% or higher (and isn't a blog), then it has issues – there is no point driving traffic to a site if it doesn't engage the visitor. There may be many reasons why a site has a high bounce rate, but 9 times out of 10, content is a key part of the problem. If existing content isn't working then it needs fixing – it also indicates that using existing messages and content to fuel PR probably isn't going to work.

- Segmenting website visitors based on where they come from and the intention behind their visit should provide a goldmine of insight for a PR. Take search. If there are certain key phrases that are driving people to a site, then using Google's free Doubleclick Ad Planner tool[32] can help determine where PR content should be pitched (it won't always be media properties that are the most fruitful places to pitch PR content – or it may disprove assumptions about which media outlets really do matter to your audiences – based on what they actually do rather than what the media owners' media pack tells you).

- Set up goals. Goals have a very specific meaning in the context of Google Analytics. They refer to very concrete, observable actions. And they don't necessarily have to be transactional. What about setting goals for time on site or depth of visit and putting a financial value on these more engaged visitors? Wouldn't it be great if a PR firm or in-house team could show a causal connection between PR activity and more engagement? Well, the tools are freely available.

- Multi-channel funnels are a recent innovation from Google and are related to the traditional digital marketing issue of 'last click attribution'. Think of the analogy of two people getting married. Who gets credit for the couple finally tying the knot? The person who first introduced them or the priest who says 'I pronounce you man and wife'? And what about all the other people along the way who helped them get to the altar? How do you apportion reward in this process? Very often the full reward goes to the last click (in this case, the priest). For example, a PPC ad results in a sale. But what about all the other marketing activity that may have helped to drive that final action? With the introduction of multi-channel funnels, Google provides the ability to see which marketing activities both impact directly and

[32]Google Ad Planner: http://cipr.co/zOwCdu

indirectly on the end goal. Being able to see how a particular PR activity assisted a conversion should be a huge bonus to the PR industry. How often have we bemoaned the fact that we know our PR efforts have had some indirect effect, but we had no means of understanding how or what? Google now provides us with that ability. We should grasp it with both hands.

PR: Public Relations or Page Rank?

At the heart of Google Search lies the concept of Page Rank (named after Google co-founder Larry Page, this remains one of the core elements of the Google Search algorithm). In simple terms, it is a measure of the authority and relevance an individual Web page has in relation to the entire number of indexed Web pages.

Why does Google rank some pages more highly than others? How many people are really searching for the keyword terms that these pages rank highly for? And why?

As we have seen, the PR sector has been generally slow to understand how SEO works. Even those that have begun touting their SEO capabilities are often doing it in a wrong-headed fashion.

If you were looking for a definition of modern-day SEO, it is about getting links from high quality, high authority sites – simple to say, but not so easy to do. What PR people generally want to know are: how do I go about identifying which high quality, high authority sites I should be targeting? And what kind of tactics are more likely to work even after I know where I ought to be pitching my content?

In this respect, the parallels between search and PR are many. Perhaps the most important is the recognition that both are involved in identifying the true sources of influence on an audience, and understanding that persuading those influential sources is not an easy task. But certainly a lot of the process can be made more effective if more effort is put into understanding how Google really works and how this impacts the way in which an organisation's reputation is filtered through the prism of Google.

In summary, I'd say Google has given the PR industry a set of tools to provide a far greater degree of insight into target audiences than we could have dreamt of in the past. These data are based on what people actually do and intend to do – rather than what we think they do or ought to do. Not only that, but Google has changed the way in which reputation is built, managed and maintained in the modern world. Given the whole raison d'être of PR (as custodians of reputation), it behoves us to get much better at grasping the true dynamics of reputation management in the modern era.

In addition, Google – directly and indirectly – is forcing the PR sector to get much better at focusing on the real measures of value: outcomes not outputs. This gives us the means to better prove the benefits of genuinely value-generating work. It would seem foolish if we did not grasp this opportunity.

Andrew Smith (@andismit) is managing director of Escherman, a specialist online PR, SEO and analytics consultancy. Smith has been a consistent PR innovator, being among the first UK practitioners to exploit email (1991), the World Wide Web (1994) and Twitter (2007). Described as the 'de facto godfather of PR blogging', he is a regular speaker and media commentator on the integration of PR with social media, search optimisation and analytics.

Chapter 4

Helen Nowicka

Digital PR that successfully factors in traditional media such as newspapers, magazines and broadcasts can achieve both broad audience awareness and more targeted engagement.

The decline of newspapers is not the death of news

The mechanics of PR have become much more complicated in recent years. Back in the 'old days' – say, pre-2005 – things were pretty much as they had been since Ivy Lee wrote the first press release[33] a century earlier, giving a rail company's version of events surrounding a fatal train crash. Put very simply, we would work up a story, pitch it to the media and if the content was strong enough, win coverage. There was a broadly unchanging network of papers, magazines and broadcasters to talk to and hence a manageable number of gatekeepers to befriend en route to reaching our audience.

How times change. First came the eruption of a new style of online reportage: opinion-led bloggers who embraced social publishing platforms like WordPress to create completely new media brands focused on their personal passion, and often with scant interest in the established conventions of journalism. Then, social networks like Facebook, Twitter and YouTube arrived, providing dynamic platforms for individuals and brands to communicate

---

[33]Wikipedia, Ivy Lee: http://cipr.co/w8835n

directly with each other and, crucially, without the intermediary of tradi-tional media. These soon went mobile courtesy of smartphones, which also introduced compelling new sources of portable entertainment like apps and games.

Suddenly, papers and magazines had to compete a lot harder for people's time and attention. No wonder publishers are having to rewrite the rule book to stay relevant, like London's *Evening Standard* abolishing its cover price to become a free product, or trade titles like *New Media Age* becoming Web only.

So, surely the writing is on the wall for 'legacy media'? Given its parlous health, as PR people, is it time to simply abandon journalists altogether and concentrate on maximising social channels? Well, actually, no and no. Granted, the sales of newspapers and magazines are in long-term decline. At £1 or more on weekdays and double that at weekends, a quality newspaper becomes a £500 + habit over a year – and in a tough economic climate people look to cut costs. Also, for many people under 30, the newspaper-buying habit has simply never been formed. No wonder that in 2010 entrepreneur and futurist Ross Dawson predicted that newspapers in their current form may cease to exist as significant entities in the US as early as 2017, and by 2019 in the UK.[34] Pulling no punches, he calls this the Newspaper Extinction Timeline.

But decline does not mean death: we are simply seeing new patterns of media production and consumption emerge. Around 9 million daily newspa-pers are still sold in the UK each day.[35] Meanwhile news websites are thriving: in December 2011 the *Mail*'s daily non-bulk circulation was 1.86 million while daily browsers at Mail Online topped 4.83 million.[36] And news-heavy talk station BBC Radio 4 regularly attracts around seven million listeners a week

---

[34]Ross Dawson blog, Launch of Newspaper Extinction Timeline for every country in the world, 31 October 2010: http://cipr.co/AnIC8j – Dawson adds: 'By insignificant I mean that non-customized mass-distributed news-on-paper will account for less than 2 per cent of media revenues. This is not a great definition for a number of reasons, but is an equivalent level to when most media and marketing people thought online was an insignificant medium.'

[35]The *Guardian* Online, Audit Bureau of Circulation, national daily newspaper circulation without bulks, January 2012: http://cipr.co/AkijCY

[36]Audit Bureau of Circulation December 2011; ABCe, December 2011.

while BBC 5 Live pulls in more than six million.[37] Meanwhile those same smartphones and tablets have become conduits for media titles to distribute their product: the *Guardian* announced around 100,000 UK downloads of its (initially) free iPad app within a week of launching in October 2011; three months later it had surpassed the half-million mark. *Metro*'s equivalent, also launched in October 2011, recorded 155,000 downloads in 11 days, while in February 2012 the *Times* reported that 119,255 digital subscribers were paying for its content across tablets, e-readers like Amazon's Kindle and the Web.

This is, without doubt, a challenging time for old media companies as they seek new business models to keep them afloat in the 21st century. While they do, as PR people, we still need to reach the widest and most relevant audience with a carefully crafted message, and traditional media remain very much part of the mix. Combine the mass awareness that they deliver with relevant touch points on digital and social channels and you have the potential to move beyond message delivery to audience engagement and advocacy.

What can traditional media do that social media can't?

To understand how best to integrate old and new media, it's worth taking a step back and thinking where their respective strengths lie. Traditional media are built around the rule that 'new is news', whether it's the latest fashion trends from Milan displayed in *Vogue* or hot-off-the-press economic data from the Bank of England in the *Financial Times*. Papers, magazines and broadcasters have historically tried to reach the broadest audience with a wide range of content in the expectation that most of their market will be interested in most of the things they report on. While there is some degree of specialisation – for instance by location (a regional newspaper or radio station) or lifestyle (a music magazine for the over-40s) – the content will still be pretty broad.

---

[37]The *Guardian* Online, Big news boosts audiences for Radio 4's *Today* programme and John Humphrys, 2 February 2012: http://cipr.co/w3leti

A lot of investment goes into creating a high quality end product, which in turn helps secure advertising. News organisations have hard-earned reputations and sizeable resources to research deep content and analysis.

Social media are highly dynamic and reactive. They don't often break major stories (although Whitney Houston's death appeared on Twitter half an hour before traditional media reported it[38]), but they can share and spread them rapidly, and will also provide a background commentary to ongoing events like the UK riots of August 2011 or the latest exploits on *X Factor*. People with a very specific interest, whether that's knitting, a particular health condition, a band or a brand, connect with each other through a range of destinations and experiences: the written word, video, audio, images. The number of people involved may range from a few hundred to several million and the majority will be content consumers led by a smaller number of content creators and curators.

That's what the media environment looks like if you dissect it from the outside. Of course the reality is that we experience it from the inside, where boundaries between traditional and social soon vanish. Tweets contain links through to news reports; blogs use hyperlinks to point readers to content off their own site; videos from one source, whether an individual or a media owner, will be embedded elsewhere. Because people experience all channels at once, the content that they read, hear or see in one environment will be reinforced when they come across it again in another. This aggregated impact is well understood by advertising agencies which develop multiple executions for the same central idea to play out over weeks and months across TV, print, outdoor, radio, point of sale and so on. PR, on the other hand, has tended to think in shorter time-frames. The focus is frequently on high impact media relations which can deliver 'here today' visibility that is all too often 'gone tomorrow'. Combining traditional and digital can extend and amplify a piece of communication beyond the quick hit of media coverage to build a deeper, and potentially ongoing, connection.

---

[38]Mashable, Samantha Murphy, Twitter breaks Whitney Houston death news 27 minutes before press, 12 February 2012: http://cipr.co/xJtLyd

How traditional and digital channels can combine

So how could this work in practice? The first step has to be developing the right overarching communications strategy that is based on a brand's business objectives. Get this right and the executional routes will follow. Second, it's important to think about digital from the start and not tag it on as an afterthought. In many agencies, and in-house too, social media specialists may not be embedded within the core PR team. These demarcations will continue to disappear as digital skills become intrinsic to the PR day job, but while they exist it's essential that all sides come together to share knowledge and agree a common starting point.

Once the strategy is agreed, the specific approaches for online and offline can be developed. Of course, these will depend on the unique communications objectives of the specific organisation. Some examples could include:

- *Traditional to digital migration* – creating content for mass media which drives people through to an owned digital presence such as a blog, game or website. Think of it as moving your audience through a funnel: traditional media coverage provokes broad awareness and interest; those who want to find out more can do so online, and the social Web can convert that interest into an interaction.
- *Community development* – as well as bringing people to a Web destination, PR content can be shared across multiple social networks like Facebook and Twitter. This is particularly effective for a campaign with an emphasis on ongoing media relations. Another approach would be a brand blog that publishes a regular diet of news for fans which is also simultaneously shared with the media.
- *Brand participation* – using PR and social channels to create something on behalf of a brand. Examples include Sneakerpedia.com, where Foot Locker invites trainer obsessives to upload photos of rare and prized sneakers to an online gallery. The simplicity of the idea and passion of the fans played out in traditional media, and during the closed beta launch period alone,

Foot Locker estimated that Sneakerpedia generated more than $ 1 million-worth of PR coverage.[39] Taking a more event-focused approach in the US, HP wanted to raise awareness of its ePrint range that will print directly from an email. A live two-hour YouTube event hosted by Rob Riggle of *The Daily Show* saw improvised comedy troupe Upright Citizens Brigade perform skits directly based on suggestions emailed by viewers to the on-stage printer. As well as attracting more than 1.2 million viewers, the event created extensive media interest with coverage in the *New York Times* and on Bloomberg TV among others.[40]

- *External relations* – airports are never far from the news agenda, and Gatwick has effectively incorporated social media into its busy press centre. It practises joined-up online and offline communications as a matter of course: for instance, when it announced its vision of how it would continue to evolve up to 2020, as well as issuing a press release and linking to it from its Twitter feed @Gatwick_Airport, CEO Stewart Wingate did a Twitter Q+A. On a day-to-day basis the feed Tweets updates on issues where Gatwick is in the news to more than 28,000 followers, while there's also a link to its blog on the media centre, putting it front-of-mind with journalists.[41] The result is frictionless media and customer relations. Other brands are also showing an increasingly integrated approach to their press offices, with British Airways, BlackBerry and Toyota all using YouTube to deliver corporate messages around issues such as strikes, service outages and faulty products instead of simply relying on traditional media channels to put their case across.

Getting closer to the gatekeepers

For PR people, a major, and perhaps slightly unsung, benefit of the social age is the way in which digital channels offer an unprecedented way to get closer to journalists. Twitter is often the environment where this happens, with

---

[39]WeLoveAd, Sneakerpedia: http://cipr.co/A6ZMrU

[40]The HP event was organised by Porter Novelli's US team shortly before I joined.

[41]Gatwick's PR agencies include Rabbit for social media and The Red Consultancy.

reporters using their personal profiles to distribute their stories or gather information. As Janine Gibson, the former editor of guardian.co.uk and now editor-in-chief of *Guardian* US, says, '*Guardian* journalists have a very complex relationship with Twitter. It's a subject of stories, a source of tips, a marketing and distribution platform, a directory, a street full of vox pops, a reading list, a tool for real-time comment and analysis, a news wire, an echo chamber.'

Custom and practice around the media's use of Twitter is evolving all the time: in December 2011 the Lord Chief Justice ruled journalists would no longer have to seek advance permission to Tweet during court cases.[42] Weeks later the BBC issued guidelines advising journalists not to break stories on Twitter before talking to newsroom colleagues, while Sky News advised its reporters to 'stick to your own beat', and not re-Tweet non-Sky content from Sky Twitter accounts.[43,44]

Today, journalists routinely produce digital content for their audiences in the form of podcasts, audio clips, videos and blogs. And news organisations are becoming more social in their behaviour too: the *Guardian* has experimented with sharing its daily news lists online, and it uses its sizeable communities to feed back on stories, thus giving readers a sense that they are contributing to the editorial agenda.

At a time when the long lunch is a thing of the past for most reporters, social media provide a way for savvy PR people to have regular, meaningful interactions with this group of opinion formers. Even better, they allow us to build relationships outside of the high-pressure time-frame of a sell-in or crisis. Simply follow journalists on Twitter, re-Tweet and interact to understand what makes them tick personally and professionally, and how they like to work. It's also worth keeping an eye on the multimedia output they're producing and thinking about how you can help by providing infographics, video or other types of handy content. And of course looking at this from the

---

[42]The Next Web, Tweet justice journalists can now live Tweet in UK courts without asking permission: http://cipr.co/zmS16k

[43]The Spy Report, UK: BBC and Sky News restrict Twitter use by journalists, 12 February 2012: http://cipr.co/AEcurA

[44]The *Guardian* Online, Josh Halliday, Sky News clamps down on Twitter use, 7 February 2012: http://cipr.co/xiekcV

other angle, reporters will be using social channels to track organisations they are interested in, so as a minimum, have an agreed escalation process to manage journalist queries that arrive via digital routes.

We've come a long way from 1906 when Ivy Lee's first press release was reprinted word for word in the *New York Times*. But in today's integrated media age, the fundamentals of PR remain relevant, as do the traditional strengths of news organisations. Both will continue to evolve at an unprecedented rate thanks to the social Web. We must embrace and engage with this evolution if we truly want to do what PR is best at: influence beliefs and behaviour.

Helen Nowicka (@Helennow) wrote for *The Times*, *Guardian* and *Independent* before joining The Red Consultancy where she worked with numerous Web brands and founded its digital team Shiny Red. A member of both the CIPR and PRCA social media councils, she's headed multiple award-winning campaigns in traditional and social communications, and became Porter Novelli's UK head of digital/ EMEA social media strategist in 2011.

Chapter 5

Gemma Griffiths

In this chapter we explore why organisations should have social media guidelines, how to create them and well-known examples of best practice. It also outlines employees' responsibility to check for updates to guidance and ensure they apply common sense and basic principles when engaging with social media on behalf of an organisation.

Definition of social media guidelines

Social media guidelines differ from organisation to organisation; one size does not fit all. That said, social media guidelines can generally be described as a set of principles created by an organisation to help employees understand the boundaries and desired dos and don'ts when engaging with social media.

The guidelines typically cover how to engage with social media on behalf of an organisation. They may also provide guidance on the appropriate amount of time to spend on social media sites during work hours, and finally, why it is essential to differentiate a personal social media account from a professional one – organisations should make it clear that posts through personal accounts that are public can be seen and may breach organisational policy if they bring the company into disrepute.

The need for social media guidelines

Despite an increase in the use and understanding of social media, many employees are still in need of guidance when it comes to social media engagement. According to a post on the Econsultancy blog in July 2011: '8 per cent of companies in the United States have fired an employee for a social media flub, while another 20 per cent have disciplined an employee for social media misbehaviour.'[45]

But these well-reported social media mishaps have not jolted all organisations into creating social media guidelines. A recent ICM Research survey[46] shows that only 24% of companies have policies for how employees should use social networking sites like Facebook, Twitter and LinkedIn (June 2011).[47]

Creating guidelines can help organisations to protect their brand online as well as empowering employees to hold conversations and spread the word about an organisation. Guidelines that create 'freedom within a framework' (a Coca-Cola phrase and concept it uses for managing its brand) are likely to yield the most positive results as they don't suffocate employees by procedure.

'Too often organisations think about social media policies as a list of restrictions. But having clear guidelines can also help employees understand ways they can use social media to help achieve business goals. For instance, policies should advise employees how they can comment on blogs or social networks to boost brand awareness and drive traffic to the company's site,'[48] comments Chris Boudreaux, a senior vice president at New York-based social-media consulting firm Converseon.

---

[45]Econsultancy, Patricio Robles, Your company needs a social media policy, 28 July 2011: http://cipr.co/AuRXh2

[46]ICM Research: http://cipr.co/wIQVf2

[47]The Brain Yard, Frank Ohihorst, Social Networking Policy: Write now or regret later, 28 June 2011: http://cipr.co/zzQCjM

[48]Entrepreneur.com, Mark Henricks, Why You Need a Social Media Policy, 6 January 2011: http://cipr.co/yDqFpR

Guidelines should not exist in isolation

Adding social media clauses into email and internet policies, confidentiality agreements or the company handbook may suffice in certain organisations as long as these policies are accessible and provide clarity on the topic.

The more clarification organisations can provide and communicate around the dos and don'ts of social media, the more chance there is of employees helping to build the brand online rather than bringing the company into disrepute.

If guidelines are created separately, it is also important that they are in line (and do not conflict) with other policies that different departments may have created.

How to get started

There are two schools of thought for creating social media guidelines. Some organisations believe guidelines should evolve over time and be drafted as and when social media opportunities and risks present themselves. Other organisations establish clear guidelines from the offset to ensure employees are familiar with the boundaries and the desired dos and don'ts from the beginning.

Most organisations opt for the latter approach. It's the safest option. The reactive approach can leave an organisation exposed and put its reputation at risk. At worst, employees could intentionally or unintentionally cause a crisis by posting inappropriate comments online or revealing competitive intelligence. Without guidelines from the offset, employees may convey different messages or communicate in a different tone, which could potentially confuse its audience and not present one company voice.

Deciding what to include in a set of social media guidelines and how much detail to go into can be one of the biggest challenges. Different organisations have different cultures, levels of desired participation, different opinions on conflict resolution and different opinions on the overall value of social media.

Here are a few areas to consider when creating social media guidelines for an organisation:

1. *Set the expectations of employees.* Define why an organisation is using social media and detail how employees can get involved.
2. *Remind employees to remain professional.* Recap on employer and employee agreements and respectfully ask employees to remain professional when engaging in social media activity. It is also useful to remind social media enthusiasts that context matters. If they are not engaging with social media on behalf of an organisation, they should state 'views are my own' on their social media profiles and should only visit these sites when not actively involved in company business – the amount of time allocated to personal browsing on social media sites is at the discretion of each organisation.
3. *Remember to include detail where appropriate.* In some cases, confusion arises because employees interpret guidelines in different ways. Some industries and organisations will benefit from providing specific advice on the type of profile pictures that are acceptable or how to respond appropriately to customers or journalists who contact employees directly.
4. *Highlight types of social media activity that need approval.* Some organisations require all social media activity to be supervised and activity to be approved and recorded. If this applies, then it will involve work outlining the approval process. For example, Profile, Background or Wall information that is usually considered 'advertisement copy' may have to be pre-approved. But real-time discussions via Facebook or Twitter may not require approval as long as activities on these sites comply with the organisational social media guidelines.
5. *Obtain buy-in from different departments and the senior team.* In many organisations social media activity cuts across different departments. These different departments should be included in the process to ensure the policy resonates throughout the company, especially the legal department.
6. *Clearly communicate the existence of and updates to guidelines.* It's one thing to establish guidelines, but they will fail if employees do not understand or know about them.

7. *Provide training.* Many instances of employees breaching social media guidelines are down to lack of understanding. Some don't realise that Twitter is a public environment for everyone to see, for example; some don't know how to set privacy settings on Facebook. Providing training sessions on how to use social media appropriately within the workplace could prevent future social media mishaps.

8. *Detail who is accountable for social media activity.* It is important to know who is responsible for day-to-day social media activity and who has ultimate responsibility for social media. It is important that employees with questions or concerns know who to consult to discuss social media activity or changes to the guidelines.

9. *Be clear about legal issues.* Make all employees aware of what is appropriate online behaviour. For example, make managers and management teams aware of employees' privacy rights.

10. *Outline repercussions of violation.* Many jurisdictions permit employers to exercise greater control over what employees are permitted to do with company equipment and email accounts, and to set reasonable policies for behaviour offline and online that is unacceptable. Being up-front and honest about these controls and outlining the consequences of not adhering to guidelines will ensure employees' and employers' expectations stay in line.

11. *Regularly revise and update guidelines.* Social media evolves at a rapid pace. Remember to continuously seek feedback from employees and peers and be ready to tweak guidelines from time to time to fit in with how your business communicates via social media.

Trust in employees

Creating social media guidelines does not guarantee that there will never be a social media mishap at your organisation. For the most part, organisations need to trust their employees and believe that the guidelines will help steer them in the right direction.

When asked how companies can keep their employees from doing stupid things online, Scott Monty, Head of Social Media at Ford Motor Company, said, 'The same way it can keep employees from doing stupid things on email and the phone. Give them guidelines and resources. Have an online communications policy that follows standard communications policies and trust them to do the right thing.'

Examples of good social media guidelines for employers

A Google search for 'social media guidelines' brings back over one million indexed pages. Here is a selection of best practice social media guidelines, including a link to a database that houses 176 (at the time of writing in December 2011) social media public policies:

- Coca-Cola Social Media Principles;[49]
- Forrester Analyst House Social Media Policy;[50]
- Intel Social Media Guidelines;[51]
- IBM Social Computing Guidelines;[52]
- Guardian Social Media Community Guidelines;[53]
- BBC Social Media Guidance;[54]
- Social media policy database.[55]

Rules of engagement for employees

For the most part, employers are responsible for creating and communicating social media guidelines. However, the onus is on employees to familiarise

---

[49]Coca-Cola Social Media Principles: http://cipr.co/z3fimI

[50]Forrester Analyst House Social Media Policy: http://cipr.co/wvDLuJ

[51]Intel Social Media Guidelines: http://cipr.co/xGYQAl

[52]IBM Social Computing Guidelines: http://cipr.co/ArrrHo

[53]Guardian Social Media Community Guidelines: http://cipr.co/xeTAMM

[54]BBC Social Media Guidance: http://cipr.co/x7QvOz

[55]Social media policy database: http://cipr.co/wfUM4Z

themselves with the guidelines, check for updates and, more importantly, take responsibility for their actions on social media sites. Often, many employees could avoid being disciplined or fired if they adhered to the basic principles of social media engagement.

Here are some basic dos and don'ts employees should consider when engaging with social media:

DO

1. **Think before you post.** Many people post views in anger or frustration. It is important for employees to remember that what they post to the social Web, for example pictures, images, Tweets, status updates (content in general), can stay online forever. Employees should take some time to think before posting and apply common sense when engaging with social media on behalf of an organisation or when engaging in a personal capacity if an account can be linked back to the employer.

2. **Add a 'views are my own' disclaimer where appropriate.** This disclaimer is typically needed if an employee uses an individual social media account to share both personal and professional opinion on matters.

   For example, it is advisable to add a 'views are my own' disclaimer to a Twitter biography if a practitioner Tweets about client and industry-related news/opinions (professional) and also shares their personal views on a subject that lies outside of their work remit (personal) through the same Twitter account. This will avoid confusion and will re-enforce the fact that an employee's personal opinion on an issue is NOT the opinion of their organisation.

3. **Correct errors openly and in a timely manner.** Always admit errors and openly 'put them right'. It is advisable to tackle an online crisis as soon as possible to stop it escalating out of control.

(Continued)

4. **Be respectful.** Always seek permission when updating information and uploading images and videos featuring colleagues or clients to various social media platforms including, but not exclusive to, Twitter, Facebook and YouTube.

5. **Check privacy settings.** Ensure personal profiles are protected and cannot be discovered by members of the public or your employers. Also, employees should not accept friend requests from managers if they don't want employers to see their status updates.

6. **Disclose relationships and connections.** If an employee is engaging on behalf of an organisation, an employee must disclose relationships with clients or other parties if endorsing an individual or a product or service.

7. **Regularly check for updates to your organisation's social media guidelines.** It is also the responsibility of employees to check an organisation's social media guidelines for updates to ensure they are always engaging with the latest guidelines in mind.

DON'T

1. **Make an audience feel uncomfortable.** It is good to be authentic and provide a hint of personality but continuously being grumpy or openly criticising people can put an audience off and deter them from engaging with an individual or organisation.

2. **Bring your organisation into disrepute.** It is likely that most legally binding contracts include a clause about employees not bringing an organisation into disrepute. It is important to remember this clause relates to online activity as well as offline activity. Refer to social media guidelines to understand the online boundaries at a specific organisation.

3. **Reveal company/client-sensitive information or intellectual property.** Offline information that should be kept confidential should not be disclosed online unless specific permission has been granted by

the parties concerned, or unless it is in the public interest or unless required to do so by law.

4. **Be fake.** Remembering to be open, honest and transparent is key to effective social media engagement. Social media engagement must be authentic. Using 'flogs' (fake blogs created by a PR agency or organisation to promote a service or product) or 'astroturfing' (the practice of falsely creating the impression of independent, popular support by means of orchestrated and disguised public relations activity) is bad practice and is likely to go against an organisation's social media guidelines. The Chartered Institute of Public Relations suggests PR professionals steer clear of these tactics.

These basic dos and don'ts for employees are loosely based on section four of the Chartered Institute of Public Relations social media guidelines.[56]

Gemma Griffiths is managing director of public relations consultancy The Crowd &I. Throughout her career Gemma has crafted and executed PR campaigns for organisations including Motorola, Adobe and LG, Wikimedia UK (the organisation behind Wikipedia in the UK) as well as start-up companies with disruptive technologies including Rebtel (mobile VoIP) and iZettle (mobile payments).

---

[56]CIPR Social Media Guidance: http://cipr.co/sm-guidance

Chapter 6

OPEN COMMUNICATION: PSYCHOLOGY, ETHICS AND ETIQUETTE

Becky McMichael

In order to diagnose social media as the solution, PR practitioners have had to develop a deeper understanding of the business problem and not just the PR objective. This has placed a greater focus on audience behaviours, ethical considerations and the etiquette surrounding the use of social media in communications.

How social media have changed the rules of PR

The broader definition of PR is how an organisation talks to, or communicates with, its audiences (the media being one channel). It is an ethos that encompasses every stakeholder touch point from product design, branding and advertising, through to sales and customer services.

Traditionally, however, PR has often referred mainly to media relations and, by implication, the audience is therefore the journalists being targeted, not the end users trying to be influenced. PR allowed the media to become the user. This disconnect is the primary cause of the current confusion and difficulty for many in PR around social media and online communications.

Evaluating the impact of a media relations campaign is built around measuring those who have read, seen or even just had the opportunity to see the media coverage. End of. No further action required.

In a social media campaign, the measurement is not around the seeing but around the doing, on both audience and PR side: Click. Like. Join. Visit.

Visit again. Sign up. Download. Order sample. Share link. Vote. Sign petition. Buy product. Recommend.

This is beyond communication; beyond education; beyond information. This is about effecting a measurable behavioural change. This is good news for PR. In an industry where measurement has been an ongoing problem, the industry is now being judged on outcomes rather than awareness or perception. But to do this rakes a much greater degree of insight and sophistication.

Social media have changed the rules of the game whilst simultaneously bringing back the practice of PR to its true definition.

The psychology behind the social media campaign

As PR practitioners have got to grips with new methods of communication, a greater focus has been placed upon understanding the business problem and objective that the client is trying to meet.

For many, the growing popularity of social media and availability of tools and case studies has meant a move away from lazy campaign planning. In the past, when a client briefed the PR agency on wanting 'to be seen as thought leaders' it was very easy to slip into a tried and tested response of 'we'll get you in the FT'.

Acting like lazy media planners, PR people have got away without developing a deep understanding of the client's business, the narrative needed to tell the story or the underlying business problem that needed solving.

During the late noughties, many PR professionals jumped aboard the social media bandwagon, diagnosing a Twitter feed or a Facebook Page as the solution to many communications briefs.

Isolated dabbling into social media has been like strapping a rocket engine onto a go-cart without any attention being paid to steering or safety. As such, it has rarely created the desired business results and, as such, has forced a change in the approach to campaign planning and measurement. Thankfully, the industry has evolved and matured, bringing with it many case studies demonstrating high profile successes and failures.

- In some cases, social media activity has failed to meet expectations or has been discontinued because of a failure to establish appropriate metrics to measure success.

- When asked to describe the value their organisations have got from social media investments, almost half of companies (47%) say 'the jury is still out', specifically because they have not been able to measure results.

- Worryingly, 42% of companies surveyed said they didn't have an ROI figure for any of the money they spent on social media. A further 23% said they could only measure ROI for a 'tiny amount of it'.

The Econsultancy Social Media Statistics Report 2011[57]

Insight-led communications

The more successful PR agencies and in-house teams have begun to approach social media campaign planning much more like advertising agencies would. The crucial difference is that the successful PR team has an understanding of the audience needs and has extensive behavioural insights into, or is actively involved with, the communities it is targeting. It can tie the creative ideas into the wider business narrative.

Where the two approaches are similar, however, is the increasing focus on the psychology of the audience. There have been many blog posts written about the psychology of social networking, mostly focusing on group participation and crowd behaviour; however, there are many other factors to consider.

As this is a social media book, it seems fitting to use the Wikipedia[58] definition of psychology as the science of behaviour and mental processes.

In order to devise a social media campaign, it is essential to explore the behaviours and ultimate business outcomes you are aiming to influence (e.g. buy Coca-Cola instead of Pepsi or buy more Pepsi) and the psychological drivers that will affect participation in the tactics you are recommending.

---

[57]Econsultancy, Social Media Statistics: http://cipr.co/wd4R1e
[58]Wikipedia, Psychology: http://cipr.co/x0aHzZ

What and why?

What is the call to action? Why should I spend my time doing it? The following checklist is a useful starting point in thinking through the possible psychological aspects of a campaign when in the planning phase:

1. What is the business problem? Who are the audience members and what are their current key behaviours? Where are they online and what is their current intent? What drives these behaviours?
2. What is the desired outcome of this campaign? What behaviour do we want to change or encourage?
3. What is our strategy and key tactical idea? Is a social media element going to reach our audience? How do we know?
4. Is the audience there on the network/community already? Do we need to drive audience or just the participation? Do we have to create the community from scratch? How does the audience use the social network currently? Does this fit with our ideas?
5. What content do we need to create? (How will we gain attention? How will we communicate when we have the audience's attention?) What else do we need to supplement this campaign with (experiential tactics, WoM, media relations, etc.)?
6. Why do we think people will participate? (How?) Is this something people will want to be publicly part of? (Are there any elements people might want private?) Is this a topic people will want to share? (How will the campaign spread?)
7. How will we make it shareable? Why will people join? Why will they continue to visit? Why will they turn participation into action?
8. What amount of action (conversion rate) can we expect from this campaign? How does that translate into results? How will we measure it?

Ethics: just because you can, it doesn't mean you should

In the previous chapter we looked at guidelines for brands, so the purpose of this chapter is to look at how PR people as individuals should approach ethics and etiquette in social media.

In an industry where social networks have enabled everybody to be a brand spokesperson, there is a need for companies and individuals alike to examine their moral compass whilst ensuring they know how to operate within the social networking world.

As with any marketing activity, there are legal constraints for social media campaigns, particularly surrounding both marketing communications across owned websites and social media properties and paid promotions within social media. Useful resources for keeping up to date with both areas are provided by the Advertising Standards Agency[59] and the Internet Advertising Bureau.[60]

However, just because something is legal, doesn't mean it is ethical, as many organisations have found out.

PR people can access a vast array of communications tools from which to harvest opinion, coverage, conversation and data but when, where and how can we use it? What is OK and what crosses that ethical line? How can we tell?

Despite greater reliance on data insights, communication is not an exact science and good judgement is one of the most valuable skills a PR officer can possess. In an industry that has always been about interaction more than one-way communication, PR should have the upper hand in the marketing industry as far as ethics are concerned.

There have been some high profile ethical failures in social media over the years, the most prominent fall into one of the following four categories and can be relatively easily avoided with proper campaign planning:

1. Offensive content.
2. Hijacking the serious news agenda (Twitter hashtag hijacking, for example).
3. Misrepresenting a brand or person, either deliberately or accidentally.
4. Taking social content out of context (scraping one network and representing content on another without permission, editing comments, deleting community activity).

---

[59]Advertising Standards Agency, Digital remit advice: http://cipr.co/AEKzVQ
[60]Internet Advertising Bureau: http://cipr.co/ySpBBB

When it comes to considering whether or not your idea or campaign is ethical, the following thought process might help:

1. Is it clear who this campaign is from, what they stand for and what they are aiming to achieve? Are any paid parties in this campaign declaring as such and is the campaign transparent?
2. Is the content suitable for the audience it is going to reach? Is the humour likely to offend anyone? Does it discriminate against any particular group? Is this intentional? Am I happy with the risk this poses? Has the content been tested on audience samples?
3. Am I sure that my campaign is not aggressive or bullying to other people? Am I benefiting from another's misfortune?
4. Am I using the data this campaign has created in a fair and honest way? Am I presenting an accurate view of the audience's response? Am I using the user-generated content in the context that it was created?
5. Am I representing myself fairly? Is my personal integrity intact? Am I answering questions honestly and representing myself or my client in an open and honest manner?
6. Am I applying common sense? Does the content represent my beliefs on my own blog or social networking page? Am I prepared to accept that not everyone will agree? Am I proud to put my name to this campaign?

The new PR etiquette

There are many guides to social media etiquette online, most of which should be considered a floor and not a ceiling for campaigns. Social networks are relatively new and, to a greater or lesser extent, the rules of engagement are still being defined by both the PR industry and the audiences involved. One thing is certain though, get it wrong and the audience will tell you, louder, faster and more publicly than ever before.

The advice often provided to clients about etiquette covers the following areas and whilst it is never applicable in all circumstances, it covers the basic rules of engagement. These are drawn from across the industry, with particular thanks to Ged Carroll,[61] Jonathan Hopkins,[62] Chris Brogan[63] and Brian Solis.[64]

1. Who are you?
   - Be yourself online;
   - Use a photo and not a logo or design – people like to see who they are talking to;
   - Fill out your biography – be open about who you work for and what you do;
   - Be careful about which account you are Tweeting/commenting from if you represent brands as well as yourself online.
2. Making friends.
   - Learn how people use social networks differently and approach them appropriately;
   - Try subscribing to someone on Facebook until you know them well enough to 'friend' them;
   - Use LinkedIn like a business card exchange – link with people after events and meetings etc;
   - Accept that people won't always follow you back – engage with them, introduce yourself and find shared interests;
   - Avoid automated response tools;
   - Find new friends and followers by content – follow topics you are interested in.
3. What you share and how you share it.
   - Consider what you share and with whom;
   - Do you really want a journalist you met once seeing photos of you in labour?
   - Do you want the whole PR industry seeing which company you are interviewing with?
   - Remember your friends may read content across a number of platforms, so don't just pipe the same stuff everywhere;

[61]Renaissance Chambara, Ged Carroll's blog: http://cipr.co/xEiqSG
[62]Middle Digit, Jonathan Hopkins's blog: http://cipr.co/AEnV4M
[63]Chris Brogan's blog: http://cipr.co/A4dJ93
[64]Brian Solis's blog: http://cipr.co/AdHaWX

- Be wary of self-promotion – make sure you promote others more than you promote yourself;
- Re-Tweeting praise about yourself makes people hate you – fact;
- Listen to feedback and change your sharing strategy appropriately;
- Don't let being unfollowed offend you – interests change;
- Gauge the volume of your broadcast and tweak it regularly – too many Tweets/statuses will put some people off, too few will leave you forgotten;
- Give credit where it is due;
- Try to add something to someone else's content before you re-post;
- Reference a friend if they gave you the idea;
- Express why you like something or what it made you think of;
- Comment on posts to give feedback;
- Reply to comments on your own posts – engagement is the name of the game, so don't post and leave.

4. Be transparent, helpful and useful online.
   - Devise a system that lets people know when you are representing a client or brand;
   - Create a disclosure paragraph or link on your blog;
   - Express how you are happy for your material to be used or shared so there's no confusion;
   - The fastest way to get content shared is to make it useful, creative and help your audience;
   - Don't be annoying;
   - Use common sense about timings, repeat for campaigns across multiple geographies/time zones, if you Tweet something at the weekend, it is acceptable to re-Tweet it in the week to capture a different audience, but don't just repeat the same broadcast hourly;
   - Don't ask for re-Tweets or follows, it looks desperate;
   - Leave space for RTs – people are less likely to RT something if they have to edit it.

5. Assume that mistakes will happen.
   - Have a strategy for handling mistakes;
   - Correct mistakes quickly and openly;
   - Risk analyse campaigns before they go live;

- Work out what criticism is genuine and what is just noise – create a filter to ensure you don't miss the former;
- Look at workflow across other customer services outlets – what happens in a store can end up online quickly;
- Don't delete content;
- Explain the error and apologise;
- Respond to critics accordingly;
- Duplicate the apology across relevant properties (the website, the FB Page, the company magazine, the Twitter Page).

People are not like you

The most important thing for anyone considering ethics and etiquette is to use common sense and treat people how you'd expect to be treated. It is important not to rely on the fact that everyone you are targeting or reaching is like you. A lot of people won't be.

Campaigns created by white, young, middle class marketers have a high risk of appearing crass or condescending at best, whilst at worst completely failing to resonate. Understanding your audience is the first step. Getting out of the echo chamber in which PR operates is the crucial second step. Do your research, test your campaigns and make sure your content is open and honest. That way, you'll always be afforded the odd genuine mistake.

Becky McMichael (@bmcmichael) has worked in PR for 14 years and is head of strategy and innovation at Ruder Finn UK. She has a BA (Hons) in Psychology and has set up a number of digital comms and community projects for both her clients and the industry. She is a member of the CIPR Social Media Panel.

Part III

Networks

Chapter 7

Robin Wilson

From its launch by a bunch of students at Harvard as a way to recognise people in the various dorms at the university, Facebook has become a global phenomenon with 800 million members as of October 2011 and numerous brands vying for audience attention. This chapter looks at how brands can use Facebook to earn audience engagement and manage reputation.

Facebook: the basics

Defined as a 'social utility that helps people communicate with people they know', Facebook is mainly used by people to share stuff with their friends, family, acquaintances and colleagues. Its founder and CEO, Mark Zuckerberg, talks about how the Facebook platform enables people to share information through their social graph, i.e. the digital map of people's real-world connections. Brands, on the other hand, use Facebook to build communities of advocates and engage with these communities using the functionality of the platform.

Facebook provides a variety of different ways to establish a presence on the network:

- *Personal Profile:* as the name suggests, this is the means by which people have a presence on the network. It allows you to share content and connect with the people you know. It's important to take control of your privacy settings so you are only sharing the information you want to share.

- *Brand Page/Profile:* organisations, brands and celebrities use Pages to engage with their Fans. Pages have functionality built in that is better suited to organisations.
- *Groups:* people and organisations can set up a Group to share thoughts and collaborate around a particular idea or cause. Groups are often used to raise awareness of serious issues, such as Raise a Child with Just One Click with four million members, and less serious issues, such as I Don't Care How Comfortable Crocs Are, You Look Like a Dumbass with 1.6 million members.
- *Places:* organisations can set up a location-based presence that people can check into (a bit like Foursquare). At the time of going to press, Facebook was phasing out the check-in functionality and making location part of the main functionality of Facebook.

This chapter will focus mainly on using Facebook Pages to engage with audiences, fans and people in general.

How brands can use Facebook

The Facebook platform is designed to enable brands to:

1. *Build communities.* Brands normally use the various Facebook 'Like' adverts to acquire Fans based on their interests and demographics.
2. *Engage with Fans.* By using a Brand Page or Profile, brands can publish interesting and relevant content to their community and engage them in two-way dialogue.
3. *Amplify your message.* Brands can amplify the social engagement of the community members, i.e. conversations with their Fans, to friends of those Fans. The logic here is that sharing how a person has interacted with a brand with that person's friends is much more powerful than standard advertising.

4. *Socially enable your business.* Using Facebook Connect, organisations can enable people to share actions they take on the organisation's website directly with their Facebook news feed.

5. *Sell your products and services.* Brands are monetising their communities by turning their Facebook Pages into shops. ASOS is leading the way with its Facebook shop,[65] where people can buy straight from the Page. The Page is integrated with the company's e-commerce system, making the experience reasonably seamless. Alternatively, some are using social shopping applications, like Payvment[66] and Shop Tab[67] – who power Coca-Cola's Facebook shop.[68] Other brands are taking a more simple approach and are putting up a shop tab that redirects people to an online shop, e.g. American Airlines[69] and easyJet.

There are some limited insights available to analyse how Fans interact with content shared on the Page. The types of data available are:

1. Basic demographics of Fans – i.e. age, gender, geographical networks.
2. Fans' behaviour – how many active users, interactions over time, which posts created the most interactions?
3. Reach and interaction – i.e. the number of post views, the number of people talking about the Page, impressions per post.

It tends to be with regard to point 2, engaging with Fans, where the expertise of public relations is most often deployed – the idea being that the more engagement a brand creates via its Page with its Fans, the more its message or content spreads through the Fans' social graphs. Facebook often cites the fact that for every Fan engaged, 120 friends of that Fan can be reached (120 being the average number of friends a person has on Facebook). Therefore, a Brand Page with 10,000 Fans can theoretically reach 1.2 million people through engagement on its Page.

---

[65]Facebook ASOS shop: http://cipr.co/z27hT1
[66]Pavvment: http://cipr.co/xprpND
[67]Shop Tab: http://cipr.co/zpNMZL
[68]Facebook Coca-Cola shop: http://cipr.co/xSRoSV
[69]Facebook American Airlines: http://cipr.co/xSLZoQ

Building a Brand Page

It's free and straightforward to create a Brand Page for an organisation. It doesn't need programming skills, as the functionality of the Page is modular. Hit the 'Create a Page' button, choose the category and add the functions you want, e.g. video, by following the simple steps given.

Once the Page is created, a number of basic tools on the Page can be used to engage Fans and spread messages through their social graph. These include:

1. Status updates – posting short text updates to all Fans.
2. Sharing photos and videos.
3. Native apps such as polls and events.
4. Custom apps – bespoke applications that create deeper engagement with the brand.

Successful engagement tends to come from authentic two-way conversations with Fans of the Page. Good examples are:

1. Oreos[70]: the brand has tapped into what people love about Oreos – the nostalgia and memories of eating the product – and regularly runs memory-sharing initiatives.
2. Red Bull[71]: the brand has created experiences and things to do on the Page that uniquely appeal to Red Bull fans.
3. Lush Cosmetics[72]: the health and beauty brand really understands what Fans like about its products and is constantly engaging with Fans in a very human way.

Many organisations opt to create a Welcome Tab, which users see when they first arrive at the Page. Using a Welcome Tab tends to be a matter of preference rather than best practice. Some Pages prefer visitors to see the Wall, where the majority of conversations occur, as their first point of contact, or a Tab dedicated to a specific initiative or campaign. It is possible to set different Tabs to be the Welcome Tab.

---

[70]Oreo Facebook Fan Page: http://cipr.co/ypExA1
[71]Red Bull Facebook Fan Page: http://cipr.co/yeOP9N
[72]Lush Facebook Fan Page: http://cipr.co/ybTVjy

Using applications

Most successful Pages use a combination of human conversations plus competitions, promotions and interactive initiatives. Facebook's rules[73] dictate that any competition or promotion on a Facebook Page needs to be run through an approved third party application.

There are a number of companies that build Facebook applications, such as Wildfire and Modern English. Apps can be complex and involved (for example using various elements of a person's Facebook profile) such as the Social Network Racer,[74] a car racing game developed by Toyota, or very simple, such as self-serve sweepstake apps, which can often be rented for less than a few pounds a day.

Facebook Offers

At the time of going to press, Facebook is testing it's much anticipated Facebook Offers product, with plans to make the feature available to all Brand Pages in the near future. Facebook Offers is the social network's latest attempt to enter the social deal space after the shutdown of Facebook Deals.

With Offers, brands can provide offers and deals, such as get one free, discounts e.t.c., to Fans of its Page. The Brand Page admin posts the Offer in their status update and the Offer appears in fans' newsfeeds. When 'Get Deal' is clicked the Offer is sent via email to the user and can be redeemed as a printout or on a mobile device.

As with other updates, users are able to share, comment and like Offers and admins can highlight and pin them to the top of a page. If a user selects a deal, privacy settings permitting, this will be automatically added to the user's timeline.

Facebook describes Offers as a way to reward loyal advocates and create engagement, actively encouraging users to connect with brands they like and would want to receive Offers from.

You can find out more here: https://www.facebook.com/help/offers# admins.

---

[73]Facebook promotions guidelines: http://cipr.co/yuL3Qs
[74]Facebook, Social Network Racer: http://cipr.co/AeKKW4

Strategies

The strategy for any Facebook Page tends to be determined by the overall marketing and communications strategies, the behaviours of the audience and objectives of the business. Most good strategies involve elements of marketing, public relations and customer service and tend to blur the boundaries between the disciplines – audiences tend not to see or care about the roles and responsibilities of the different disciplines, they just want to talk to the organisation.

Social media industry analysts Josh Bernhoff and Charlene Li stated in their book *Groundswell* that a good way to create a strategy is to think about how the organisation wants the relationship between itself and its audience to change.

There is no one single way to plan a strategy for a brand's Facebook presence, but it is good to think about the following when planning:

- *Audience.* What does the audience do in social media – upload content, rate and review products or watch videos? Forrester's social technographics research is a useful way of profiling audiences' behaviour in social media.
- *Goals.* Define what you want the Page to achieve, how it fits into the overall marcomms plan and set the KPIs.
- *Rules.* Ensure that any internal or external industry rules and regulations are factored into planning. For example, with alcoholic drinks marketing, it is against the Portman Code to show people who look under 25 in marketing materials – which could impact on a strategy that involves users uploading photos.
- *Conversation strategy.* What is the desired relationship between the organisation and the audience? What is the desired response from the audience?
- *Content plan.* Devise a plan of content with which to engage the audience. This could be a weekly, monthly or quarterly plan depending on the strategy and content available.
- *Operations.* Who will manage the Page? What will be allowed and not allowed? Develop response protocols for crises and reputation issues.

Useful examples

There have been a number of high profile examples of great uses of Facebook for particular campaigns:

- *Ford Explorer.* Ford created an industry first when it launched its new car – the Ford Explorer – exclusively on Facebook. It streamed the launch live to its Facebook Page, ran a competition to win the car and built a widget where users could create their own car. The campaign was supported by paid media and PR. Overall, Ford[75] is a great example of how to use Facebook effectively.
- *Papa John's Pizza.*[76] The US pizza company asked its Facebook Fans to come up with a new pizza for the company, where the winner received a share of the profits from the sale of the new pizza.
- *Mad Men ad of yourself.*[77] Via a Facebook app, Don Draper and his team take details from your Facebook Profile and from it create a Mad Men ad.

Facebook and reputation management

While Facebook can be a great way to build and engage communities of advocates, it can also be the source of negative sentiment that damages a brand. People can easily set up Groups and Pages to express their dissatisfaction towards an organisation. They can directly comment on and even attack an organisation's Facebook Page. For example, Nestlé's KitKat Facebook Page was the target of an activist attack protesting against the company's use of palm oil in KitKats.

However, if done well, a Facebook Page can be a great tool for managing a crisis. An organisation can quickly and easily take control of its messaging and communicate directly with its audience. Via the Page, it can immediately answer questions, tell the company's side of the story and minimise the

---

[75]Ford Facebook Fan Page: http://cipr.co/xIsvAj
[76]Papa John's Facebook Fan Page: http://cipr.co/AfrjrX
[77]Vimeo, Mad Men Ad: http://cipr.co/AbBha9

spread of mis-information. It is worth pointing out that an organisation needs to have an existing community on Facebook for crisis management to be effective. Trying to build up a community to manage a crisis is usually not successful.

Evaluation

Like all social media, the evaluation of Facebook campaigns is a heavily discussed topic. At the time of going to press, there was no dominant industry standard for Facebook evaluation. Taking the lead from traditional PR evaluation methods, Facebook campaigns can be evaluated by looking at:

- *Conversation triggers:* the number of status updates, comments, photos and so on that the organisation will post to the Page to generate conversations.
- *Conversations created:* the number of Fans of the Page and the number of Likes, comments and posts by those Fans.
- *Conversation outcomes:* this measure is tied back to a business objective or marketing objective and could be anything from increased sales to reduced customer complaints, depending on the aims of the Page and how it fits into the overall marketing strategy.

In general, the goals of the Facebook Page should support the goals of the organisation and, ultimately, be evaluated against those goals.

Overriding thought

Facebook is used by many types of organisations to do a variety of things – from selling more products and managing customer service to creating positive sentiment and communicating useful information. The most successful uses of Facebook all tend to have a few things in common: defined goals, clear strategies and a thorough understanding of what appeals to the audience.

Robin Wilson (@robin1966), social media director at McCann Erickson Manchester, has more than 20 years' PR and social media experience, representing brands including Apple, Durex, Facebook, Motorola, MTV, Symantec and Yahoo! He was lucky enough to launch the iPhone in the UK, head up the Facebook agency's corporate comms team in the UK and launch Yahoo!'s social search engine, Yahoo! Answers. At McCann Erickson, Robin directed the Durex Play O campaign – which won the CIPR Excellence Award for the Best Use of Digital in the UK in 2009.

Chapter 8

Alex Lacey

Less than six years after launching for public use, Twitter has become an unavoidable communications tool. There is almost no area of public life upon which Twitter has not had an impact, and it is this meteoric and unexpected rise of influence that has made it such a powerful platform. This chapter explores how this has come to be; how Twitter has fundamentally changed the way we consume news, interact with organisations and celebrities, and why it can't be ignored by any organisation that has a relationship with the public.

Twitter may well have won the battle for dominance, but when it launched in July 2006, it was just one of a range of microblogging platforms all competing for a share of the space. The new concept of ultra-short-form blogging was no more than a toy for those looking for the next big thing, and few people nowadays use or even remember the likes of Jaiku, Plurk or Pownce.

The core concept of microblogging itself has changed very little since that time. Twitter describes itself as 'a real-time information network that connects you to the latest information about what you find interesting.' Additional functionality has been added by Twitter itself as it became clear that it had cornered the microblogging market, but equally clear that to survive it was going to have to become a revenue-generating business.

Twitter really began its rise to dominance in 2007, at the annual music, film and interactive conference South by South West (SXSW) in Austin, Texas, when it won the Web award in the 'blog' category. After this, Twitter fast became the microblogging platform of choice amongst technology-savvy

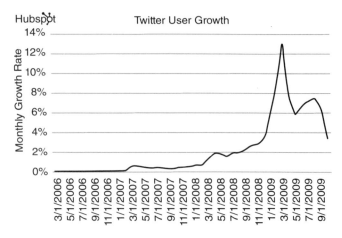

Source: HubSpot[78]

early adopters. Shortly afterwards, the platform began to garner interest amongst the celebrity Technorati. Both Stephen Fry and Ashton Kutcher were particularly influential in this respect, when they began mentioning the site during media interviews or on their blogs.

Twitter and journalism

The real-time nature of Twitter has had a profound effect on journalism. In 2009, one user Tweeted posts and pictures from the US Airways 1549 aeroplane that landed in the Hudson River in the US. The user's Tweet said, 'There's a plane in the Hudson. I'm on the ferry going to pick up the people. Crazy.' This was the first time Twitter broke a story before a major US broadcast network.

In many cases, journalists no longer monitor newswires, but use Twitter instead. At a recent conference organised by the Chartered Institute of Public Relations (CIPR), Carla Buzasi, Huffington Post's UK editor-in-chief, pointed

---

[78]HubSpot blog, Rick Burnes, Twitter User Growth Slowed From Peak of 13% in March 2009 to 3.5% in October, 19 January 2010: http://cipr.co/ycUXVP

out exactly this, saying that of the two screens which all her editors use, one is always dedicated to trending Twitter topics.

Naturally, this has to have an impact on the way public relations (PR) professionals engage with journalists, pitch stories and release their news. Twitter provides PR professionals with an opportunity to gain insight into how to influence their community, individuals or organisations, and the way consultants work with the medium has to reflect this.

Twitter as part of a communications programme

To many, the value of Twitter is overly simplified. It's a way to get closer to your favourite celebrities, or get better access to relevant and up-to-date news, or even just a new alternative messaging service to chat with a group of friends. Indeed, the majority of Twitter members are pure consumers of information, not participants. According to GigaOM, '80 per cent of Twitter users have Tweeted fewer than 10 times, and 40 per cent of users have never sent a single Tweet.'[79]

The truth is a lot more complicated, as evidenced by the number of both national and global Twitter-led stories over the past three years. At its simplest, its impact can be viewed within one of two main concepts – either engaging or transformational – and when a communications project aims to incorporate Twitter into its arsenal, it has to be clear which of these it's trying to achieve.

Twitter as an engagement tool

As an engagement tool, Twitter is largely self-referential and conversational. It will either aim to help a brand serve its public better, or it will try to engender greater loyalty by creating a closer tie between the brand and the consumer of that brand.

---

[79]GigaOm, Colleen Taylor, Move over techies: Students are taking over Google+, 19 August 2011: http://cipr.co/xaIBMI

This may sound ephemeral, but there are plenty of examples of Twitter being successfully used in this way all the time, both in business and in entertainment.

Arguably the most widespread daily use of Twitter for engagement is that of the once unidirectional medium of television. News, current affairs and entertainment shows encourage users to share opinions through the relevant hashtags, making it easier to see and engage with other viewers in real time. This interactive process generates a much closer bond, and therefore loyalty, for the consumer to the programme by making it personal and relevant.

From a business perspective, some of the potential uses of Twitter became readily apparent when companies saw how people were using Twitter to discuss products they'd bought, or challenges they were facing. More so than any other online tool, Twitter has provided a personalised outlet for customer feedback on products and performance. Companies utilising their '@brand' name can listen to, respond to and interact with anyone who chooses to have an opinion on their products. Clearly this isn't restricted to product development either. In the same way that complaints about a product can be damaging when spread online, they can also generate an opportunity for positive engagement. This sort of thing is seen all the time when @JohnSmith Tweets, 'Loving @brand customer service which just sorted my problem minutes after I posted my complaint. Would recommend to everyone!'

Of course, the other natural area for Twitter to become integral to modern communications is that of brand protection, or more specifically crisis management. As with anything in crisis management, it's not without its risks, but bad news spreads rapidly these days, and people demand information faster than ever before. Twitter's real-time nature has only increased this pressure. This can be an excellent way of protecting your brand, but more importantly, if you're not dealing with the crisis on Twitter, someone else will be, as BP discovered in April 2010. It's widely accepted that the spoof BP Twitter account, @BPGlobalPR became disastrous for BP when it effectively took control of the company's public communications. Less than two months after the disaster, the stream had more than ten times the following of BP's official account, @BP-America.

Twitter as a transformational tool

Only when engagement has become successful can Twitter become transformational. Generating engagement with a target audience can quickly lead to increased influence. When an audience can be influenced by a brand or an individual, their behaviour can be changed, and Twitter starts to become a tool for transformation, not just engagement.

When this change happens, brands and individuals need to be prepared, because it can go wrong. The perfect example of the entire process can be seen in Ashton Kutcher's Twitter evolution up until November 2011.

At the time of writing, Kutcher has over nine million Twitter followers. In April 2009, he challenged CNN, one of the biggest TV news channels in the US, to a race to become the first account to reach 1 million followers on Twitter, and on 16th April he won. Kutcher said, 'I found it astonishing that one person can actually have as big of a voice online as what an entire media company can on Twitter.'[80]

Unfortunately he also didn't fully appreciate the influence and accompanying responsibility this had given him. In November 2011, in response to Penn State (a US football team) coach Joe Paterno being fired, Ashton Tweeted, 'How do you fire Jo Pa? As a hawkeye fan I find it in poor taste,' along with the hashtags #insult and #noclass.[81]

Kutcher was almost instantly bombarded by thousands of Tweets asking why he was supporting a football coach who was being accused of sexually abusing children. By all accounts, he was said to be mortified, as he had not been aware of these facts before publishing his opinion on the case.

Kutcher was forced to reconsider how he Tweets as he realised Twitter was no longer just connecting him to his fans; he had become a credible source of information – an influencer – to his followers. He handed control of his Twitter account over to his management and PR team. He commented, 'While I feel that running this feed myself gives me a closer relationship to

---

[80]CNN Online, John D. Sutter, Ashton Kutcher challenges CNN to Twitter popularity contest, 15 April 2009: http://cipr.co/vZAyz8
[81]CNet News, Chris Matyszczyk, Ashton Kutcher freezes his Tweets after Paterno pratfall: http://cipr.co/yMA2Vk

my friends and fans, I've come to realize that it has grown into more than a fun tool to communicate with people.'[82]

The amount of transformation that Twitter continues to drive is truly astounding – on both a national and a global scale. The instant and public nature of the medium allows for real-time genuine citizen journalism, from wherever the user is. The 2011 'Arab Spring' represented one of the first times that Twitter was used as a mass medium to gather worldwide public support for the political and humanitarian plight of the Egyptian and Libyan populations. It is universally accepted that it was the struggle of these peoples that led to a change of regime in those (and other) countries, but there can be no doubt that Twitter played a vital role in the international support that accompanied them.

Twitter can draw people's attention to an issue and gather support for it faster than any other tool. Pressure and lobbying NGOs such as Avaaz and 38 Degrees have been using it successfully for years to drive support for petitions against legislation, and this in turn has led to a greater role for the tool within the wider political arena. As arguably one of the most influential politicians on Twitter, West Bromwich East MP Tom Watson has found a great deal of use in the service to drive support for both his parliamentary lobbying around anti-digital rights bill legislation and, more famously, his campaign against illegal journalistic and editorial practices at News International publications.

Twitter versus Facebook

Twitter and Facebook are often seen as the poster children of social media, along with Google of course. But, it's worth noting that, apart from the obvious differences in features and functions, there are also differences in how people engage with the two platforms.

Users on Twitter have a different mindset to users on Facebook. Users on Facebook are more inclined to virtually wander around the site looking at

---

[82]Wired, Lewis Wallace, Ashton Kutcher, Don't Be a Twitter Quitter!, 10 November 2010: http://cipr.co/xPqfmG

videos, pictures and comments that are of interest to them – they are in discovery mode.

Users on Twitter, however, are slightly more frantic. They are more likely to share links or re-Tweet posts and video links but are less likely to actually click through and watch or read the articles, according to a study conducted by Mashable in March 2011. The study looked at the Mashable users' social data and how many people read articles they posted to Facebook compared to how many people read articles posted to Twitter.

Mashable's study went on to reveal: 'Twitter received roughly 0.38 clicks per Tweet, whereas Facebook received 3.31 clicks per engagement (the number of times people posted a Mashable link to Facebook through an action on a social plug-in or through a Wall post). This would mean that a Facebook action gets roughly 8.7x more clicks than a Tweet.'[83]

Whatever the future for Twitter, there is one key point that businesses should take to heart: it's here, and is going to happen whether or not you're involved. Any company that might have dealings with people in the public sphere in any way (including business-to-business companies) can only influence the outcome of this if they have a presence on Twitter. Regardless of the engagement you're trying to achieve, owning and managing the '@brand' name is a vital part of managing modern online brand appearance.

> Alex Lacey (@Lexlacey) has run PR campaigns for a range of established global brand names, including Hewlett-Packard and BT, for more than 14 years. For the past three years, his focus has been on harnessing the potential influence offered by over 50,000 distributors across EMEA in the highly regulated nutritional supplement environment at Herbalife.

---

[83]Mashable, Vadim Lavrusik, Is Sharing More Valuable for Publishers on Facebook or Twitter?, 25 March 2011: http://cipr.co/yUAD2O

Chapter 9

Matt Appleby

Often seen as Facebook's sensible older brother, LinkedIn doesn't get the same attention as more headline-friendly networks. But it's a lot more than a place to host your CV and meet recruitment consultants. Could you benefit from expanding your professional network?

Even as it comes within a year or two[84] of celebrating its first decade, opinion is split between those who hold LinkedIn up as the senior social network, the 'grandfather of social networks',[85] and those who maintain 'LinkedIn has never been a "social network" '[86] or that 'LinkedIn was sort of Web 1.0's version of a social network.'[87]

By the CIPR's definition of social media, it certainly ranks highly as a popular network for 'the building of communities or networks and encouraging participation and engagement'.

---

[84]LinkedIn About Us: http://cipr.co/xLUSCJ

[85]CIPR Conversation, Stephen Waddington, CIPR Summer Social: the LinkedIn special, 14 September 2010: http://cipr.co/zFGGRe

[86]CIPR Conversation, David H. Deans, Why Few Marketers Reap the Full Potential of LinkedIn, 6 August 2011: http://cipr.co/wuW74B

[87]Brian Solis and Deirdre Breakenridge *Putting the Public Back into Public Relations*, FT Press, 2009, ISBN 978-0137150694.

'Over 135 million professionals use LinkedIn to exchange information, ideas and opportunities',[88] says the site's UK homepage and, as of November 2011, there were more than six million members in the UK.[89]

The numbers definitely suggest it should be taken seriously as a platform with significant reach in professional networks. As the site has increased the types of interactions available (moving away from being a 'Web 1.0' network), it is lining up to compete more directly against the other major social networks for marketers' attention.

The gradual addition of features such as Twitter integration, LinkedIn applications and company status updates in recent years has made the network increasingly social, adding features which all enable and encourage greater engagement between members and companies.

Whereas advice to LinkedIn users has traditionally focused on capitalising on the individual opportunities it presents, companies increasingly need to stay alert to how these developments will impact on their social media strategies.

The more that LinkedIn adopts social features, the greater the need for it to be managed at a corporate as well as an individual level. It elevates the need to build a relevant, engaged following on LinkedIn to the same importance as the bigger beasts of Facebook, YouTube and Twitter.

As with all networks, companies need to ensure that they have a clear strategy and objectives for engagement through LinkedIn, that they have identified the groups and conversations which are relevant to them and that they have the resources and policies in place to manage their participation in those conversations.

LinkedIn has certainly become established as the leading professional social network, doubling its membership in the UK over the last two years. While other newer networks (particularly Google+) may be waiting in the wings to challenge its position, it continues to establish itself as arguably the most important online platform for business-to-business engagement and communication.

---

[88]LinkedIn: http://cipr.co/zrYx8w
[89]LinkedIn About Us: http://cipr.co/xLUSCJ

What's in it for me?

'Senior level executives use the site mainly for trade industry networking (22%) and promoting their businesses (20%). Middle managers are more likely to use LinkedIn primarily to keep in touch (24%) with others, as well as for industry networking (20%). Entry level employees, not surprisingly, are using the site mainly for job searching (24%) and co-worker networking (23%).'[90]

LinkedIn sells itself as a platform to connect/reconnect, boost your career and find answers; simple really – just an online extension of our offline networks.

So what's to get excited about? In 2010, LinkedIn had two billion people searches and it's on track to double that in 2011.[91] A complete LinkedIn profile with a custom URL set-up is also likely to appear near the top of any search for your name (go on, Google yourself).

If you're in a position where being easily found online is an advantage – and there aren't many people who aren't – then there's a clear, compelling argument for taking your personal LinkedIn profile seriously.

In *Online Public Relations*, Phillips and Young[92] point to our human desire to seek society 'in different groups, different types of groups...for different purposes and different "selves"'. They argue that in PR this usually means we should look to belong to a large number of groups, rather than broadcasting in groups with large numbers of members.

LinkedIn gives us this opportunity to belong to multiple networks based on school, university, employer, shared skills, professional bodies, shared interests, local business networks and so on. It's the ideal platform for identifying and connecting with people across multiple niche groups.

Essentially, it's a highly effective tool for managing a personal professional brand online. If you do nothing else – no blogs, no Twitter, no podcasts or

---

[90]CIPR Conversation, David H. Deans, Why Few Marketers Reap the Full Potential of LinkedIn, 6 August 2011: http://cipr.co/wuW74B

[91]LinkedIn About Us: http://cipr.co/xLUSCJ

[92]Phillips and Young *Online Public Relations*, CIPR PR in Practice Series, Kogan Page, 2009, ISBN 978-0749449681.

videos – LinkedIn gives you a platform to be found and to create a professional online presence.

As well as a showcase for your personal achievements and those who recommend you, there are multiple opportunities to build an authoritative voice – particularly useful to smaller businesses and consultants. It's easy to demonstrate expertise through Answers, Skills, Polls and Group management or discussions.

The site continues to launch new tools to add to this list. The Alumni platform gives you quick access to make connections with university classmates or find new contacts in businesses who share your alma mater. The Skills tool (in beta) is a useful way to showcase your skills under established keywords within your profile and also to find others with shared or relevant expertise.

One recent study found that 75% of US companies will always or sometimes check out a prospective employee's online profile.[93] The surprising thing about this statistic is that it isn't 100%.

The trail we leave behind us online is crucial to the success and development of our careers – it has to be positive and in the case of LinkedIn, the starting point is the fullest possible profile. We want employers, colleagues and clients to be able to easily find content that shows us in the best possible light.

This is even more important for PR 2.0 professionals. As we carve out a new role, genuinely participating[94] on a personal level in the communities with which we seek to engage, we are constantly blurring the line between 'PR person' and 'person'. We are expected to participate openly – whether on our own behalf or for our employers/clients – exposing ourselves to greater personal scrutiny. We will be judged on the impact of our personal blogging, recruited on the basis of our social media following and valued against the online company we keep.

Authenticity and transparency play a critical role in our effectiveness and LinkedIn is a vital tool in ensuring we communicate the professional side of our identity as part of our wider online personality and profile.

---

[93] Jobvite Social Recruiting Survey May/June 2011: http://cipr.co/wlHveb
[94] Mark Brooks: 'You ARE the company these days…You can't hide behind a brand any more.' (quoted by Deirdre Breakenridge *PR 2.0*, FT Press, 2008, ISBN 978-0321510075).

It's also why automatically linking your social networks together is not advisable – you don't necessarily want your weekend Facebook photos or your Twitter rants waiting for you on your LinkedIn status on Monday morning. It's easy enough with the #in tag to mark only those Tweets which you want to share through LinkedIn.

'Conversations among human beings sound human'[95]

While Facebook may be the king of branded Pages,[96] LinkedIn has been developing its corporate offering since the launch of Company Pages in November 2010. Within a year, two million companies have created LinkedIn Company Pages.[97]

What Facebook has become to consumer marketing, LinkedIn is for business-to-business. 'LinkedIn is strictly business, and that's what makes it such an attractive option for business-to-business marketers.'[98] And we know that top executives turn to the internet for business-related information more than any other source, even recommendations from colleagues or friends.[99]

So the introduction of more truly social features to LinkedIn's Company Pages should be a game-changer for the site and for marketers' ability to bring business-to-business brands to life.

The original Company Pages enabled members to follow, share and see who in their networks was linked to the business or had recommended its products and services. There was careers information and a tab to showcase specific products. The major change in November 2011 – the addition of company status updates – is a major shot in the arm.

---

[95]Levine, Locke, Searles, Weinberger *The Cluetrain Manifesto*: http://cipr.co/w6oILi
[96]The impact of Google+ branded Pages has yet to be seen at the time of writing.
[97]LinkedIn About Us: http://cipr.co/xLUSCJ
[98]Gillin and Schwartzman *Social Marketing to the Business Customer*, Wiley, 2011, ISBN 978-0470639337.
[99]Forbes in association with Google *The Rise of the Digital C-Suite* 2009 (referenced by David Meerman Scott *The New Rules of Marketing and PR* 2010): http://cipr.co/xlYhAb

As LinkedIn moves more closely to resemble Facebook in pinstripes, it has added familiar engagement tools. Company updates to followers now appear in their profiles. They can Like, Share and Comment – creating what LinkedIn calls a unique conversation with your company. And any interactions can be seen by members' networks, expanding their reach to a much wider audience. All of which you can keep tabs on and manage through Page Analytics.

For the PR person, these are developments which have significantly increased the importance of LinkedIn within the development and delivery of our social media strategies.

LinkedIn also says that Company Pages present an opportunity to reveal the human side of a company, to see the individuals behind the brand and highlight how people use its products.

This is interesting in the wider context of how companies benefit from their staff's activities on LinkedIn. There are clear benefits to using the Company Page, but every employee is also both ambassador and advocate with every connection and interaction they make across the network.

One of the most memorable of *The Cluetrain Manifesto*[100] theses is: 'We know some people from your company. They're pretty cool online. Do you have any more like that you're hiding? Can they come out and play?'

What more natural way to humanise corporate communications than to let people out to play – particularly when there's a purpose-built playground for them?

The Groups network has a niche for almost any business need – and the facility to start your own if you can't find what you want – with user-friendly discussion and sharing tools built in. Through Answers, members can benefit from the shared knowledge of their network or showcase their own expertise by helping others.

Both allow companies to share the talents of those they employ while also giving people outside the business more direct access to those within. There's a clear reputational benefit here, as well as demonstrating an understanding of social media best practice, increasing the porosity of the business and enabling it to speak in a genuinely human voice.

---

[100] *The Cluetrain Manifesto*: http://cipr.co/w6oILi

How do you make it work either for you or your company? The golden rule of social media engagement applies here: what do you have of value to the community that you can share? As Todd Defren puts it, 'think random acts of content'.[101]

PR professionals have always been skilled in helping businesses to identify the news/content that they have (or could generate) and then crafting it into something of interest to others. There is a valuable role for us to play in supporting strategic engagement through LinkedIn, both at the corporate and individual level. As well as engaging in our own right, of course.

Finding inspiration is a bit of a struggle as there aren't many great case studies out there. LinkedIn's marketing solutions site has plenty of high profile examples[102] of success stories which are a good start. The Company Pages for those businesses who were first out of the blocks on launch day – Dell, Microsoft, HP, Volkswagen and Philips – are all also exemplars of what can be achieved.

Where next for LinkedIn?

By deliberately mirroring 'real life' networks, LinkedIn is a simple site for businesspeople to use and its value is immediately clear. Setting up is easy and the social features are familiar to anyone who has used any of the other major networks. LinkedIn wants to help you make the most out of the system and its Learning Center is a real strength, with easy-to-follow guides tailored for everyone from students and job-hunters to companies and journalists.

Gradually adding company-specific facilities and supporting social commerce have increased the importance of the site to business-to-business marketers.

But as I write, Google+ has launched Pages. It looks like a swipe at Facebook, but there's a real potential threat to LinkedIn. The Circles concept – easily segmenting contacts/friends into multiple groups – enables you to keep social and professional separate but manage them together in a single

---

[101]PR Squared, Todd Defren, *Brink* e-book: http://cipr.co/xUGnTR
[102]LinkedIn Insights and Case Studies: http://cipr.co/zzKOxP

network. And for businesses it will integrate with Google Docs, Analytics, Search and YouTube for starters.

The real killer may well be Hangouts – a simple, free group video conference facility with masses of applications for everything from project collaboration to face-to-face customer service. So, after a few false starts with social networks, Google is competing strongly in attracting members to Google+ in its early days.

Crystal ball time, then – where could LinkedIn go next?

Video is clearly key to the future of social media and LinkedIn is already offering it as part of company status updates. But an offer which competes with the Hangouts concept would give executives even greater value from using LinkedIn to connect with their network.

LinkedIn is increasingly accessed with mobile devices and here there are clearly opportunities for innovation. For example, adding location-based check-in functionality which enables you to see LinkedIn contacts nearby and displays their pictures and profiles – no more remembering a face but not a name at business events. Or how about the ability to scan a conference hall with a LinkedIn-augmented reality app to recognise faces and overlay profile details or show your mutual contacts?

Wherever it goes, it continues to develop its social media and social commerce functionality. To the uninitiated, LinkedIn may look like it lives in the shadow of the cooler consumer kids, but a reach of six million UK professionals (and counting) is a pretty compelling argument to put it centre stage in any business-to-business campaign.

Matt Appleby FCIPR (@mattappleby) is managing director of Golley Slater PR, Wales and leads its UK social media arm GolleyEngage. He blogs about food, edits a hyperlocal community news site and is active in the Cardiff bloggers and Social Media Surgery networks. Matt is a CIPR Chartered PR Practitioner and a former chair of CIPR Wales.

Chapter 10

Dan Tyte

When Google announced its new network, the world sat up and signed on. But after the botched Buzz, and ubiquity of rivals, could the community be a plus for PRs? With the power and presence of the Tsar of Search, it's hard to argue not.

After all the column inches and social chat around the launch of the latest attempt at stealing the social space from the Mountain View monolith, you could be forgiven for thinking Google+ had hired a very good PR team.

In a year dominated by headlines of revolutions, royal weddings and red top scandals, the new network was widely reported on upon announcement of its field trial in the summer of 2011. And why wouldn't it be? After all, Twitter had created a new verb for tabloid hacks to learn, so when the digital deity Google got back in on the game, people rightly sat up and took notice.

The rhetoric from Google was as altruistic as we've come to expect. On the official blog, Senior Vice President of Engineering Vic Gundotra, posited that although our lives had moved online, the 'subtlety and substance of real-world interactions' had been 'lost in the rigidness of our online tools. In this basic, human way, online sharing is awkward. Even broken.' Fear not, though, because the good people at the search supremo were here to save the social network.

While Facebook's 800 million+ active users and Twitter's 100 million microbloggers might have had something to say about Gundotra's grim claim and gung-ho counter-claim, he had a point – a very good point. Take a look at your Facebook 'friend' list – go on, now. I know you're online. My guess is school friends and work colleagues sit alongside distant cousins, the guy you met at the Full Moon Party, an ex-girlfriend's brother and often your boss, or even your mother. Surely only the unsubtle would say or share the same content in these circles?

Which is exactly where Google's big idea for its new network comes in: Circles. In a thinly veiled dig at Mark Zuckerberg's contribution to anthropology, Gundotra claims that 'today's online services turn friendship into fast food'. And again, he's kind of right. How many of your Facebook 'friends' are actually your real-life friends at this present moment in time? Google+ was promising functionality to be able to segment your online contacts into groups according to the nature of your relationship. So you could create a friend circle, a family circle, an acquaintance circle, a foodie circle, a football-lover circle, a media circle, a PR circle, a client circle. You could even circle the squares you knew!

Google's thinking was that insensitivities and social niceties stopped us sharing. Existing online communities were a bit like weddings, with everyone we've ever known under one roof. This clubbing together of contacts made us mind our Ps and Qs – or cuts and pastes – but split circles would bring an end to this pussy-footing. Users could now share content safe in the knowledge they wouldn't be upsetting Auntie Rita with stag do pictures or looking sappy in front of soccer team-mates with love limericks to long-lost sweethearts. So far, so good.

Invites to the restricted-use 90-day field trial were like golden tickets for geeks. PR practitioners were at the front of the queue. Okay, so Facebook does have friend lists which essentially do the same thing, but they're clunky and not at front and centre of the service. With Google+'s circles, audience segmentation, and the implications this had for delivering specific messages to specific groups was promised within a click. The PR world licked its lips.

But before we all get ahead of ourselves, can I refer you back to the much-maligned Google Buzz? The network was launched in a blaze of glory just one year previously, and billed by executive Sergey Brin as 'bridging the gap between work and leisure'. In October of 2011, and after an ill-conceived privacy setting shared users' most mailed contacts with others, Google announced it was closing the service, but not before being taken to court for revealing information on a woman's workplace and partner to an abusive ex-husband.

So after the shenanigans of Google Buzz, would Google+ turn out to be hollow hype? Could it really fix the alleged 'broken' way we shared online? Would the verb 'to Google+' enter the pages of the *Oxford English Dictionary* in 2012? Would the PR world be revolutionised?

Does the + outweigh the −?

After Google+ left beta testing and opened up to the great unwashed in September 2011, data from Experian Hitwise showed that usage skyrocketed by 1269%.[103] Okay, well that's to be expected. But still, site visits of 15 million – although paling against Twitter's 33 million, YouTube's 530 million and Facebook's 1.8 billion – were impressive enough. But PR people know it's easy enough to get people to the opening party. The question is, would they be wowed enough to become regulars?

First things first, what does the party look like? If you're already a Gmail user, like close to 200 million of us are, then things are pretty good. The Google+ profile is integrated into the top right-hand of your inbox, with updates easy to spot and the all-important 'Share' button the equivalent of a neon sign on Broadway. But these days, we're rarely at our desktops. We want to share on the tube, at the track or in the crowd at the football or festival. What's the Google+ user experience like on the go?

With mobile such a vital part of modern PR strategies, it's no surprise Google made apps available for iPhone, Android and other leading mobile platforms pretty sharpish after launch. On an iPhone, the stream of updates can be swiped from people already within your circles to posts from 'nearby' users. A cursory glance at mine at the time of writing finds a call for the people of Canton in Cardiff to re-post an update to find a 'missing tortoise-shell cat'. While I hope Tiddles makes it home safely, take a second to think about the opportunities for brands, particularly in the service industry, to listen to, learn from and engage with their communities.

---

[103]US figures, week commencing 17 September 2011.

Which brings us to brands. At the time of writing, Google+ hasn't quite got its head around the integration of brands into the community. Understandably, companies are champing at the bit for a shop front in the newest mall in town but to date the Plus Police have 'kicked out tens of thousands of brands'[104] from the network. Anecdotal evidence told us that several brands had been approached by Google to be part of the initial wave of ware-peddlers to have their passports stamped. In November 2011, the walls came tumbling down, and the opportunities for organisations from the local bike shop to FC Barcelona (one of the first to get their own Page) could outweigh even those of Facebook.

Sure, brands love Facebook. And why wouldn't they? There's 800 million fish in a barrel to shoot at. But advertisers don't have it all their own way – post-click engagement tracking, search inefficiencies and limited customisation have had some users dreaming of a better way. Facebook doesn't allow advertisers to track post-click engagement of non-Facebook ads which post users to Fan Pages, leaving a glaring grey area over all-important return on investment metrics.

Google+ is already at an advantage. Facebook trail-blazed the way brands and users interacted online, and, like all innovators, had to break a few eggs to make the omelette. Facebook was never intended to be a brand platform and the inefficient and annoying way commercial concerns used the Group function for so long confirms that, online, Rome wasn't built in a day. If Google+ can learn from its predecessor's mistakes, it's already one nil up.

With the major chunk of the search market, it's almost inevitable that the search opportunities for Google+ brands should outweigh other networks. The Facebook.com domain has a relatively low click-through rate (CTR) and subsequent low quality score in Google's auction-model. The knock-on is higher cost per click for paid search ads driving to Facebook as opposed to a brand domain; a problem when so many consumer-facing brands use their Facebook Pages as proxy home pages. It doesn't take a genius to assume that Google+ Brand Pages are going to be better regarded by Google's search engine and hence more cost-efficient to brands.

---

[104]Google+ Product VP Bradley Horowitz, August 2011.

Add to that the fact that if Google integrates its detailed Analytics into evaluation of Brand Pages (and as with search, why wouldn't it?), then the ability to be able to factor the myriad of metrics into how Pages look and talk would be a cut above the current options open to organisations. Real-time data on time spent on Page, visitor loyalty and percentage of new visits could make Google+'s Brand Pages uber-optimised. And Facebook's Analytics, although improved, still lag some way behind.

Power to the PR

So, Google+ could be better for brands. But how can its other features help PRs? We've already chewed the fat over the super-segmentation potential of targeted wastage-free messages through Circles. Fortunately, that's not the only exciting opportunity for communicators.

We PRs know the key to communication success is relationships. Get to know your audience, understand what makes them tick, tock and go to the shop. Learn to love journalists who can make a difference to your campaign, and do your utmost to ensure the feeling is reciprocated. How many times over the past few years have you put the phone down to a hack and instantly searched for their Twitter profile online? If you're like me, literally thousands. And how many times have you become closer to them through Twitter talk and reaped the coverage benefit? Again, if you're like me, literally hundreds (and if you're not, why not?).

In November 2011, Google announced that journalists' profiles will start being highlighted in Google News. But instead of flagging up their profile from their primary website (or their publication's), it's their Google+ profile which will be linked to their article. When the journalist has a Google account linked to their article, their profile picture, general information, link to profile and an 'Add to Circles' button will pop up. The databasing and message management possibilities of this feature will be a huge plus for anyone working in PR.

It's all well and good to be linked online, but every PR worth their salt knows there's nothing better than the old school opportunities that arise from face-to-face meetings. Google+'s hip-named Hangouts could well become the way we, well, hang out, in the not-too-distant future. But more than that, the video chat capabilities enable users to invite whole Circles into video conferences. It won't be too long before we start to see Hangout hack briefings to Circles of relevant writers or focused focus groups to a Circle of product testers around the world. Google has added features like Google Docs integration, sketchpads and screensharing to make the service even sharper.

What first seemed like Google+'s 'Like' equivalent, the +1, now seems to be more of a social network sharer like Delicious. With code available to add the button to the stories on sites, PRs should be grabbing the opportunity to make their stories shareable on the newest network out there. After all, you wouldn't ignore a newspaper with a relevant audience for your press release would you?

While it's not there yet, the possibilities presented by Google+ could make the day-to-day business for PRs more efficient, exciting, enlightened and effective. When Vic Gundotra argues that with so many internet users already using Google for other reasons, they'll eventually find their way to Google+, it's hard to see past that logic. And with Google's search and analytic power behind it, the case becomes more compelling. Okay, so maybe not all of the 40 million+ users are active yet, but make sure you're part of the first wave and the pluses will far outweigh the minuses.

Dan Tyte (@dantyte) worked in PR pre-social networks and has run campaigns for professional sports teams, pop musicians and alcoholic drinks using on- and offline tools. A director at Working Word and committee member of CIPR Cymru, Dan is writing a novel, set in a PR and digital agency, saved of course in Google Docs.

Chapter 11

Stephen Waddington

Blogging has become a significant chapter in the story of media fragmentation and the emergence of social media, seeing individuals and organisations become publishers of their own content, effectively creating their own media properties.

The internet has ravaged and rebuilt almost every industry that it has touched, none more so than the media industry. In time we'll almost certainly come to see the invention of the internet as being as significant to civilisation as the printing press in the 15th century. The printing press enabled documents to be reproduced with scale, removing the limitation of manual copying. The development of the internet during the late nineties, and with it the launch of consumer dial-up services, meant that anybody could publish content, initially text and photos, and later audio and video, to a global audience. The cost of entry was basic Web publishing skills and space on a Web service. And so the blog was born.

Blogs typically focus on a particular topic or industry and are usually maintained by an individual, or small group, with text, photo and video content published in chronological date order. Most are interactive, allowing visitors to interact with the blogger via comments. In this sense, blogs were one of the first forms of social media, providing a means of interaction between the publisher of the content and the audience. Now blogs typically include options to share content via social networks such as Facebook, Google+ and Twitter. This enables a blog to build its audience via other social spaces.

Where a blog is run by an organisation, it is typically clear who is responsible for the blog and a policy will stipulate whether the opinions are personal to the blogger or the views of the organisation publishing the content. Internet and software companies were quick to spot the opportunity to simplify the process of publishing content and created content publishing systems and hosted Web services. Services such as Blogger[105] from Pyro Labs (launched in 1999 and purchased by Google in 2003), TypePad[106] (launched 2003) and WordPress[107] (launched 2003) allow content to be published on the internet in a blog format. More recent additions include Posterous[108] and Tumblr.[109]

Initially, in the late 1990s, blogs were used by individuals to publish their comments or opinions, but quickly became recognised as a means to engage directly with an audience. By 2004, blogging had started to become a mainstream communications activity. Politicians, business professionals and journalists started to use blogs as a means of communicating their expertise, achieving the benefits below:

- *Direct engagement* – executed well, blogging provides the means to build and engage with an audience in a participative environment around an issue or topic.
- *Leadership and social capital* – publishing content on an area of expertise either by reporting on events or sharing authoritative comments means that a blogger can quickly become recognised as an expert.
- *Search engine optimisation (SEO)* – content published regularly using the best practice Web publishing format of a commercial blogger platform is an excellent way of attracting the attention of Google around keywords.
- *Raw Web traffic* – blogs can be designed to attract the attention of Google around keywords or social strategies that engage an audience via networks such as Facebook and Twitter to generate traffic.

---

[105]Blogger: http://cipr.co/Aces35
[106]TypePad: http://cipr.co/zR6gk5
[107]WordPress: http://cipr.co/ybboim
[108]Posterous: http://cipr.co/xiljAt
[109]Tumblr: http://cipr.co/xiFZkg

- *Call to action* – posts can include a call to action to prompt the reader to engage directly in a transaction with the blog. You could invite your audience to download an e-book, attend a seminar or buy a product directly.

The relationship between blogging and search marketing is well proven. Blogs with headlines, body text and tags provide a search-friendly format for posting content. By using basic search planning techniques and a keyword strategy, bloggers can drive significant amounts of Web traffic.

How to start blogging

Setting up a blog is a straightforward task. It will take you less than five minutes to configure a basic template. Head online to any of the commercial blogging platforms already cited and register an account. Blogger and Word-Press are the most popular platforms. These are both managed services where the blog is hosted on a server provided by the platform. This means that the services are robust but the potential for the customisation of anything from the look and feel to the URL is limited. WordPress produces a self-hosted service for installation on a Web server that overcomes these issues. It is more complex to configure, typically requiring technical support, but enables every aspect of the blog to be customised.

Once a blog has been set up, you're ready to post content. Blog platforms typically have some form of online text editor into which the user either types directly or pastes text that has been cut from a word processor document. Photos and videos can also be inserted or embedded by grabbing a snippet of Web code from a third-party site such as Flickr[110] or YouTube.[111] Herein is an issue with posting content to a blog. There is no sub-editor to proof or check content for taste, decency or quality. Inevitably many blog posts are published containing grammatical errors and spelling errors which are off-putting for the reader who may not return to the site. Blogs produced on behalf of a

---

[110]Flickr: http://cipr.co/yVQFal
[111]YouTube: http://cipr.co/xDKhLG

commercial organisation often introduce a process to ensure that content is checked prior to publication.

Generating content is an editorial process. A good start point is to investigate the keywords that are likely to bring Web traffic to your site. Consider drafting blog posts which directly address questions that your customers ask. Reviews, opinion, comment and guest blogs are all good tactics for developing content. Read other blogs and media outlets for inspiration. It is worth developing a content calendar to ensure that you're always thinking about the next blog post.

How often blogs should be posted to is the question most often asked at blogging workshops. As often as you are able to post original content is the typical answer. Once a week is good as a kick-off, but more frequently is even better. Posting regular, engaging content builds traffic and an audience. You should blog as frequently as you want people to pay attention to you. Although still in its relative infancy, blogging has developed in two ways, both of which provide opportunity for the public relations industry: the majority of blogs are published by individuals who generate content around an area of expertise, then there are blogs or networks of blogs produced by an organisation, typically on a topic aligned to the products or services of the organisation.

Bloggers as individuals

A blog on a particular subject or topic will not be hard to find, however niche or specialist. Head to Google Blogs Search[112] or Technorati[113] and hunt around for an area of interest. You'll almost certainly find hundreds of blogs, whatever the topic. Parenting, food, technology and travel are among the most popular topics, with hundreds of bloggers posting regular content, often to a sizeable audience.

As the media fragment, bloggers have emerged as an influential audience online. The PR industry has been quick to spot the opportunity to work with bloggers in the same way that it has worked with traditional media. Bloggers

---

[112]Google Blog Search: http://cipr.co/xFxOhg
[113]Technorati: http://cipr.co/wDEg2c

provide an opportunity for third party editorial validation and a means to reach an audience. The result hasn't been the easiest of relationships. The issue is that PR practitioners have expected their media relations skills to be directly transferable to bloggers. They aren't. Bloggers typically fit writing around a full-time career or are motivated by their own interests. According to the Technorati State of the Blogosphere Report 2011,[114] two-thirds of bloggers write about brands and report that they are approached up to eight times per week.

Engaging with bloggers

Herein is the challenge for PR practitioners in working with bloggers. There is no standard approach. Standard pitches must be avoided at all costs. Blog-by-blog research is critical to understanding the motivations of a blogger. Some bloggers do accept content on the same basis as journalists, but more often bloggers refuse PR pitches of any kind, preferring to discover their own sources of content. Others are happy to blog about an organisation if it is willing to sponsor a post. Google Blogs Search or Technorati are the most basic means of identifying bloggers around a topic. Beyond that, emerging blogger communities such as the Tots 100 UK Parents Blog Index,[115] run by Sally Whittle, provide PR agencies and brands with access to their networks for a nominal fee.

Business blogs

The second opportunity for the public relations industry is to create blogs as a form of branded media content on behalf of an organisation. It is no surprise that personal blogs were quickly followed by a rush of businesses quick to adopt this new communication format to publish corporate content. But the personal nature of blogging seldom translates well to the business

---

[114]Technorati State of the Blogosphere Report 2011: http://cipr.co/xKnxop
[115]Tots 100 UK Parents Blog Index: http://cipr.co/wnQoU3

environment. Good commercial blogs are hard to find because of the organi-sational and communication challenges of the genre.

Blogging was going to change how organisations communicated with their audiences forever. A revolution was set to sweep through corporate communications. At least that was the view of a *Business Week* cover article published in May 2005. PR and communication teams would cease to exist as business leaders used the Web to communicate directly with their audi-ences. Blogs promised to fundamentally change the relationship between a company and its staff, customers, suppliers and the media. Websites would be overhauled, the press release would cease to exist and the PR industry itself faced revolution. We're still waiting.

It's an overstatement of the case of course, but five years on there are very few examples of large organisations – outside the media, information and technology industries – that have successfully used a blog as part of their communication strategy. As a rule, good corporate blogs are hard to find, but here are some that you should check out:

- Asda – Your Asda[116] tells the back stories behind the business and the people and products within its stores.
- CIPR – the UK's Chartered Institute of PR uses a blog format[117] to issue news announcements and engage in conversation with members.
- Dell – Direct2Dell[118] is one of the oldest business blogs. New products and deals are released via the site and Dell staff use it to discuss issues pertinent to customers.
- PayPal – the online payment merchant uses the PayPal Blog[119] to discuss product developments, mobile payments and issues relating to its business.

One of the reasons that there are few examples of good corporate blogs is because of the clash between personal and corporate communication. The

---

[116]YourAsda: http://cipr.co/zQ83ca

[117]CIPR Newsroom: http://cipr.co/sm-newsroom

[118]Dell Community Forum: http://cipr.co/xPDrRi

[119]The PayPal Blog: http://cipr.co/yOyWIG

typical life-cycle starts with an initial burst of two or three posts per week, dropping to one a week, then one a month before drying up completely. Blogging isn't a short-term marketing tactic. It takes time to establish a blog, develop a tone of voice and build an audience. There are fundamental differences between how people communicate and how companies communicate – and very few corporate organisations have managed to bridge that gap.

Then there is the issue of ownership. Should a blog be the pet project of a senior executive or fall within the communications or PR team, product marketing, customer relations or human resources? And legal will almost certainly want to get involved and pass judgement on blog posts and comments. Finally there is the issue of the generation of authentic content. It's the only way to attract and stimulate an audience, yet organisations see it as time consuming and requiring the constant input of senior management.

Stephen Waddington MCIPR (@wadds) is the co-author of *Brand Anarchy*, published by Bloomsbury in March 2011. He co-founded Speed, the UK agency at the forefront of helping brands such as The Associated Press, *The Economist*, Tesco and Virgin Media Business manage their reputation in traditional, online and social media. He sits on the PRCA Council, the CIPR Council and is a member of the CIPR's Social Media Panel.

Part IV

Online Media Relations

Chapter 12

Stuart Bruce

Public relations has changed dramatically since its birth in the early part of the 20th century. Does the humble press release still have a role in the 21st century or has it been totally superseded by 140-character pitches on Twitter and video pitches on YouTube?

On 28 October 1906, Ivy Lee, one of the founding fathers of modern public relations, issued the world's first press release on behalf of the Pennsylvania Railroad, following a major train crash. It met with widespread acclaim as the Pennsylvania Railroad was seen to be keeping the public, media and officials well informed. From that glorious first moment the humble press release has fallen from grace. It is now often derided by journalists who are 'spammed' with hundreds of releases a day, often with no real news or even relevance to that journalist's beat.

Almost 100 years later on 27 February 2006, ex-*Financial Times* journalist Tom Foremski wrote a devastating critique of the use and abuse of press releases entitled 'Die! Press release! Die! Die! Die!'

> 'Press releases are nearly useless. They typically start with a tremendous amount of top-spin, they contain pat-on-the-back phrases and meaning-less quotes.'

The response from the online public relations community was enormous and the blog post received hundreds of comments and spawned dozens of other blog posts and news articles. It is now even cited on many university public relations courses. Within days, Todd Defren, principal of USA-based Shift Communications, had created and issued a news release based on the ideas in Foremski's blog post.

On 23 May 2006, Shift Communications published the world's first social media news release template and made it '100% open to the PR/marketing community.' It wasn't just small PR firms that were taking notice, as in June 2006 Richard Edelman, CEO of Edelman, announced that it would be releasing its own version of the social media news release. In December 2006 it launched StoryCrafter, an in-house tool to enable Edelman to create social media releases for its clients.

It didn't take too long before all of the major commercial newswire news release distribution companies started to launch their own versions of social media news releases for use by their clients. Some of the major players in social media news release distribution include PR Newswire, SourceWire, PRWeb and RealWire. Another benefit of newswire distribution services is that they automatically get the release featured in various news syndication and aggregation sites, including Google News. The actual sites vary from service to service.

Some of the discussions and called-for improvements in social media releases aren't actually to do with the 'social' element at all, but simply about the need for better news releases. A good news release should be free of marketing spin, factual, newsworthy and well-targeted, regardless of whether it is a social media news release or a traditional one. Despite this, a huge number of news releases, if not the majority, are still of very poor quality.

The next logical step after social media news releases was the modernisation of the traditional online pressroom that many companies used as a static repository for their press releases. The social media newsroom essentially contains all of the elements of a social media news release, but also acts as an archive and hub for even more content.

Essential elements of a social media news release and newsroom

Since the launch of Shift Communications' original social media news release template there has been much work to develop, refine and improve the social media news release by organisations such as the Social Media Club and the International Association of Business Communicators (IABC). The author of this chapter was one of the first PR professionals in Europe to work as part of the Social Media Club to develop the format and issued the UK's first social media release in September 2006.

Despite all this work there is no definitive definition of the essential elements of a social media release and, as befits the rapid evolution of the social Web, the elements are constantly updating and changing. The commonly accepted essential elements are:

- *Headline* – this should be written for both humans and computers, so it needs to tell both a compelling story and contain the right keywords for search. The ideal length is 90–120 characters (including spaces) as this makes it easier to share on Twitter and Facebook and can be rapidly scanned as an email subject line.
- *Introductory paragraph* – should tell the whole story and that might mean the classic who, why, what, when, where. It's critical that it conveys the main message and should also be interesting enough to entice the reader further.
- *Supporting paragraphs and/or bullet points* – Shift's original social media news release template advocated using bullet points to convey the main facts of the story. I'm firmly of the view that well-written traditional prose is still the better option.
- *Anchor text links* – a good social media news release will be written to include lots of anchor text links. This is where keyword-rich phrases or words are linked to another relevant page on the internet. For example, a news release on the launch of a new mobile phone would include the phrase 'sharpest mobile screen' and link to a specific page on the company's website that has information on the phone's screen. This serves two purposes: one is to provide the reader with easy access to additional information and the second is that it improves the search engine optimisation of the release.
- *Quotes* – unlike a traditional news release a social media news release can include multiple different quotes, providing journalists and bloggers with a selection to choose from. The additional quotes are often broken out into

a separate section after the main news release. Quotes shouldn't just be company management, but should ideally include staff actually involved and responsible for the subject of the news releases as well as third parties such as customers, analysts, academics, etc.

- *Supporting facts* – the internet makes it much easier to provide all of the sources of facts and claims in the news release. This might include links to the original research or survey, links to other expert sources or links to additional information on the company's or third party websites.

- *Multimedia* – a selection of audio, video and images that can be used to illustrate and enhance the story. Instead of just providing one picture or video, a social media news release can provide a wide choice of images and videos that can be used. Instead of just having some written quotes, it could include an interview with a spokesperson or a video demonstration of the product.

- *Infographics* – there has recently been an explosion in the use of infographics, with widespread use of them on blogs and mainstream media. In fact, infographics are not new; one of the world's best known is the London Tube map, which was designed in 1931 by Harry Beck. An infographic is a visual representation of information, data or knowledge. Infographics are often best used to help illustrate research or survey results.

- *Social network sharing tools* – make it easy for the reader to share the news release by including buttons for sharing on social networks such as Facebook and Twitter.

- *Email sharing button* – 43% of all news sharing happens on social media and social networks, but email is still how many people choose to share interesting news.

- *Social bookmarking tools* – include buttons for people to share and save the news on news aggregation communities such as Digg and StumbleUpon as well as social bookmarking sites like Delicious.

- *Links* – as well as providing links to supporting facts, it is also useful and helpful to include links to other related media coverage and even competitor information. If a journalist or blogger is going to research the topic anyway, it is better for them to use your news release as their central hub or resource as they are going to be able to search for and find the information anyway.

- *Creative Commons Licence* – some companies still carry dire warnings on their online newsrooms that the content is for 'media use only', thus dissuading bloggers and citizen journalists from using them. A Creative Commons Licence is a form of online copyright release which makes it clear how the content can be used and shared.
- *Contact information* – as well as providing traditional contact details such as the media office phone number, mobiles and email, it should also provide contacts via Twitter and instant messaging tools such as Skype, Microsoft Live Messenger and Google Chat. It can also include links to profiles on LinkedIn, Facebook and Google+ for both the public relations contacts and the spokespeople quoted in the release.

Another important element of the social media news release is that it is not 'sent out' in the sense that a traditional news release would be emailed or faxed to journalists in its entirety. Instead it is intended to be discovered via search (pull public relations as opposed to the traditional push) and to be pointed to by circulating a link to relevant contacts using both traditional email and other social channels such as Twitter and Google+. That's another reason why the headline and introductory paragraph are so important, as, often, that is all the recipient will see.

The social media news release can then be hosted on the Web as a standalone page, on a newswire distribution site or on a dedicated social media newsroom.

A social media newsroom will consist of a collection of news releases containing all of the above elements, but should usually have additional ones such as:

- *RSS* – nearly every online news site and blog includes an RSS (Really Simple Syndication) feed to enable readers to subscribe to the content without needing to constantly visit the site. At the very least a social media newsroom must contain an RSS feed for all of its content, but it is better to tag and categorise news so that it is possible to subscribe to just certain types, for example corporate or product. The very best newsrooms enable users to create their own feeds of just the news categories they are interested in. Services like Google's FeedBurner add analytics and extra functionality to the RSS feed, including the ability to subscribe via email.

- *Image gallery* – traditional online pressrooms usually included a limited selection of photographs and corporate logos, but a social media newsroom enables a much wider selection to be made available. Instead of hosting the photographs directly on the corporate website, the social media newsroom can embed a gallery from Flickr or Picassa. Hosting the photos on a public photo-sharing website makes them easier to search for, reaches an additional audience of that site's users and makes it easier for people to actually use the photographs on their own blogs or social profiles.

- *Video gallery* – hosting video on a corporate website used to involve a lot of network server space and required a great deal of bandwidth because of the large size of the video files. Now it can be easier and more effective to host the videos on video-sharing sites like YouTube and Vimeo. In addition, many corporate videos no longer need to be television quality and can now be shot and edited directly by the public relations team, all of whom should have been trained to produce video in the same way they were once trained to produce traditional print newsletters.

- *Search facility* – it is essential that the social media newsroom contains a good search tool to enable visitors to quickly and easily search for the information they require without leaving the site.

- *Tag cloud* – tagging news releases with relevant keywords not only makes them more search engine friendly, it also enables you to provide a tag cloud so visitors can quickly see the types of news contained on the site and filter it to match their interests.

- *Coverage archive* – provides links to and showcases previous online coverage. This can be done by creating a manual list on a Web page or using a social bookmarking service like Delicious.

- *Spokespeople* – as well as providing biographies, contact details and links to online profiles for corporate spokespeople, the social media newsroom can provide a way to search and filter them according to their specialist topics.

- *Corporate calendar* – key events from the corporate calendar should be listed on the social media newsroom. If this is done using an online calendar service such as Google Calendar or Windows Live Hotmail Calendar, it enables visitors to subscribe to the calendar on their own online calendar service, desktop diary program like Outlook or smartphone.

- *Background information* – a traditional online pressroom would have contained a selection of 'backgrounder' documents on the company, its products and services written from a factual viewpoint and free of the marketing hyperbole to be found elsewhere on the corporate website. A social media newsroom provides an ideal hub to host, publish and distribute a much wider variety of corporate information including annual reports, research reports and data, white papers, etc. Uploading this collateral to document-sharing sites like Scribd or Edocr improves their search ranking and makes it easier for people to share them. Repurposing documents into presentations also enables them to be uploaded and shared on SlideShare, further improving their search ranking and the number of ways people can find your company information.

Another benefit of social media newsrooms is the flexibility and ease of use of the content management system, meaning that the PR team can quickly and easily upload news releases, even from smartphones, without the need for any support from the IT department.

Originally the only way to create a social media newsroom was to build one from scratch using either the existing content management system on the corporate website or by integrating an independently hosted site on the same domain. The two best content management systems for creating social media newsrooms are WordPress and Drupal because they both feature lots of independent third party plug-ins that provide functions such as Flickr photo galleries, bookmarking and social sharing buttons.

Today there is also a burgeoning market in software as a service for social media newsrooms, where companies provide a hosted solution that can be customised and branded to suit different requirements. Two of the leading players are PressPage and MyNewsDesk, but there are many others to choose from.

Using a social media newsroom to its best

One of the benefits of a social media newsroom is that it can be used as a publishing platform in its own right. This means it can be used to publish content that is intended for customers, investors or other stakeholders rather than just being for journalists. This means that the investment in time and resources that goes into creating news releases is maximised, as the audience is no longer just a few journalists, but all stakeholders.

This also means a company can choose to publish news and features that it thinks will be of interest to some of its stakeholders, but might not be of interest to the news media and journalists.

This is a technique that has been used very effectively by First Direct, which launched the UK's first financial services social media newsroom in 2009. It not only contains First Direct's normal news releases, but is also used to publish stories about its community relations and charity activity. Some of these stories, which have never been directly pitched to journalists, have subsequently been used as the basis of mainstream media articles. Shortly after the launch of First Direct's social media newsroom, the number of visitors it received increased to about 2400 a week compared to just five or ten a week for its old online newsroom.

One of the first companies in Europe to create a social media newsroom was GM Europe; it was soon followed by Electrolux and Philips, which became the first company in the world to launch a multi-language social media newsroom for the four languages of its Nordic companies.

HSBC, parent company of First Direct, used First Direct's experience to launch its own social media newsroom in September 2011. The HSBC press office has successfully integrated its use of Twitter into its social media newsroom and has set up two Twitter accounts for interaction with journalists, bloggers and other online influencers. The @hsbc_uk_press account is for personal finance, while the @hsbcukbusiness account is for business banking. The new social approach to news has already proved its worth, enabling HSBC's press team to respond rapidly to a crisis that occurred on a Friday afternoon when all of HSBC's computers went down, leaving consumers unable to use bank cards or withdraw money from ATMs. Much of the interaction with journalists took place on Twitter and a statement was rapidly published on the social media newsroom.

Social media news releases and social media newsrooms should not be seen as a panacea on their own. They will only work if they are coupled with a new approach to modern media relations which means learning to interact with journalists and online media in new ways. The modern media no longer just need a good story, but are also looking for interactive and multimedia content. The public relations professional must become more data driven and analytical in identifying news and content opportunities.

Stuart Bruce MCIPR (@stuartbruce) has worked in PR and corporate communications for more than 20 years and, in 2003, started one of the world's first PR blogs. He has created social media newsrooms for companies such as Philips, Sony Ericsson and First Direct. He has also counselled global companies like Unilever, PayPal and GSK on modernised media relations and online corporate communications strategy.

Chapter 13

Rob Brown

With the advent of the social Web, brands have been able to publish content, be it news, information or rich media, more effectively than ever before. Some brands are emerging as publishers in their own right.

Corporate publishing and brand journalism

To a partial extent brands and businesses have always been publishers. The public relations function has acted as a primary conduit, conveying news and information from organisations to their various stakeholders and audiences. Historically, company newsletters, annual reports and a range of other print media from leaflets to magazines were common platforms for delivery of the PR programme.

The relationship between brands, media and publishing goes back a long way, certainly well before the arrival of the internet. The television soap opera is a staple of modern-day viewing but little thought is given as to why recurring drama series are called 'soaps'. The moniker comes from the drama serials broadcast originally on radio in the early 1950s which had soap manufacturers like Palmolive, Lever Brothers and Procter & Gamble as sponsors. More recently, supermarket retailers have been title publishers for quality consumer magazines.

As a broader range of media have become democratised and deliverable through the Web, it should come as no surprise that corporate bodies have taken the opportunity presented to them to communicate in new ways. The first tentative steps into a richer media world are traceable to the 1990s, when the corporate website became a possibility. For the majority of brands and organisations, the websites were static and more akin to digital brochures than media channels. The increasing prevalence of content management systems allowed the corporate website to become dynamic. This opportunity to publish more created an innate demand for content and narrative. Brand journalism emerged as a term to define this narrative.

The definition of brand journalism is widely debated, but the concept emerged as much from the advertising world as it did from the PR industry. In 2004 Larry Light, McDonald's' chief marketing officer, challenged the power of mass marketing, declaring that, 'no single ad tells the whole story' when he announced that McDonald's would be adopting 'brand journalism' as the foundation for its future marketing strategy.

'We don't need one big execution of a big idea. We need one big idea that can be used in a multidimensional, multi-layered and multifaceted way.' He defined brand journalism as explaining 'what happens to a brand in the world.' David Meerman Scott, author of the best-selling *New Rules of Marketing and PR*, argues 'brand journalism is when any organisation – business-to-business company, consumer product company, the military, nonprofits, government agencies, politicians, churches, rock bands, solo entrepreneurs – creates valuable information and shares it with the world.'

The commercial benefits of publishing

There are powerful business reasons for brands to act as media. For the majority of organisations, the traffic that comes to their website via search is commercially valuable. Google and other search engines favour dynamic content. If a website is dynamic, it will be favoured by search engines and by definition, if you are publishing on a regular basis there will be more content that is searchable. Behaving like a media channel is a way of drawing more attention to your site and therefore to your brand.

A real challenge to commercial operations, unused to working this way is that if they are going to operate as media channels then they need to think and act like them. Some organisations have realised this and like the German venture capital company Rocket Internet, actively hire editors and content managers. Perhaps the simplest way for an organisation or a brand to create its own media outlet is to have a blog. Companies like Kodak, Dell and Coca-Cola were early adopters of the corporate blog. The forms are many and varied, from daily diaries of the chief executive to a glorified press release channel. Many organisations have taken this relatively straightforward step to gain direct contact with the customer and consumer.

A genuine trailblazer in understanding the value of publishing for a commercial organisation is the US retailer Whole Foods Market. The organic supermarket has not always had a flawless relationship with the social Web. Its founder and CEO, John Mackey, was investigated by the US Securities and Exchange Commission. *The Wall Street Journal* revealed Mackey had been using a pseudonym to add posts to Yahoo Finance forums criticising rival supermarket chain Wild Oats and praising himself and the management of Whole Foods Market. He attempted to promote Whole Foods $670 million acquisition of Wild Oats through this bogus identity. The SEC investigation cleared him and the deal eventually went through. Perhaps scarred by this experience, Whole Foods Market undertook a radical overhaul of its entire Web presence, including Facebook and Twitter (where it has more than two million followers). The core website feels like a home interest publication specialising in recipes and organic food. The content is easily accessible and updated all the time. Traffic statistics place the Whole Foods Market website in the top 1500 US sites. In the same period, Whole Foods Market has experienced continual growth and expansion. In 2005 the company joined the Wall Street Fortune 500 and rose to position 273 in the 2011 listing.

Other retailers around the world have embraced the idea that creating media channels around their brand is good for communications, their relationship with customers and ultimately for the business. In 2010 leading UK supermarket Asda's chief executive Andy Bond said, 'All of our businesses are supported by a world-class customer engagement programme that is taking advantage of the rise in social media to enable us to get even closer to our customers'. The chain created the YourAsda blog and, during the 2010 UK general election, broadcasts from all the major political party leaders including Gordon Brown, David Cameron and Nick Clegg were published via the AsdaMums forum.

Video and television

There are certain sectors that particularly lend themselves to engaging through new media channels. The gaming industry clearly enjoys a high correlation between the people who use its products and people who spend a high proportion of their time connected and online. One of the most popular and successful YouTube channels is EA Vision, the channel created by gaming giants Electronic Arts. It even has its own flagship series 'PWNED', a gaming magazine show featuring trailers, interviews, the latest updates on games in development and behind the scenes insight. The series has been created with the production values of a mainstream broadcast television series and its highest viewed episode reached an audience of more than 1.5 million. This is a classic example of directing high quality media content that is of particular interest to a niche audience.

The famous Australian lager Fosters has broken new ground by acting as a broadcaster with its own dedicated comedy video channel. Fosters has commissioned series from popular comedy actors and programmes with proven track records like Steve Coogan as Alan Partridge, Vic Reeves and Bob Mortimer and the cult *Fast Show*, which had been off mainstream television for fourteen years. New original series are made available exclusively online under the Fosters TV brand. The channel, which is accessible either directly or via YouTube, also contains Fosters own comic advertising, allowing the brand to entirely bypass conventional TV broadcast channels. Their strategy has been extremely successful, garnering seven million views in a year. Admittedly that figure could be achieved in one evening on a mainstream television channel, but it is still a mass communications exercise and one that has been achieved by the brand exercising total control over the means of delivery.

A role for public relations

The emergence of the concept of brands acting as media channels has gone hand in hand with the growth of the idea that the media landscape from a marketing perspective is divided into three groups: paid, owned and earned. Historically we had paid media, which were the domain of the advertising world, and we had earned media, which were largely represented by editorial coverage, most often in the charge of the public relations function. The social Web has facilitated the emergence of a third media group that organisations can own.

There is a further important driver for brands operating particularly in niche sectors to create their own media channels. We continue to see pressure on, and disruption of, conventional media models. What historically constituted the advertising media budget is now distributed across a greater range of activities. Not only is part of this money being used to fund owned media channels, it is being spread more thinly across fragmented broadcasting and spent on digital campaigns that include elements like search engine optimisation. With their advertiser-funded model failing, conventional publications are closing and this can create gaps in the market. Some narrow industry sectors are no longer served by trade publications and therefore brands have to act as publishers simply to continue to communicate with their stakeholder audiences.

The emergence of the Web has undoubtedly created opportunities for brands to reach audiences in new ways, with new narrative content. In some sectors this creates an imperative to participate whilst for others it provides new options. Where brands choose to develop owned media channels and operate as publishers, it is essential they understand the challenges. Public relations has an important role to play. The PR adviser has always had to determine whether a piece of content has inherent value. Is it interesting, is it compelling, is it news? With new direct routes to publication, the temptation will be even greater than it ever was for a brand to communicate something because it is interesting to those most closely involved, irrespective of whether it holds any fascination for a wider audience. The editorial role of the public relations function is therefore more important than it ever was. The problems aren't limited to the challenge of creating interesting content.

Risks and reward

As with any engagement with the outside world, there are risks and examples to show where organisations have got things badly wrong. Take the Tesco-owned 'fresh & easy' chain in the US, which posted the following to its corporate blog:

Pausing for breath at fresh & easy

Phew! We've opened 31 stores in 66 days so far this year...now we're pausing for breath. We've been delighted with the openings. There's always been a line of customers waiting for each store to open. Indeed at some, such as Long Beach pictured above, the lines were almost too long, they took hours to clear – I'm sorry if anyone was inconvenienced. And every week, we attract more customers in our existing stores. However, after opening our first 50, we planned to have a 3-month break from openings, and other than a couple more in Phoenix, we're taking it (albeit, in our usual fashion, with 59 stores already open).

This seems open and honest, but it told the market something that it did not know, which, combined with the hint that the store-opening programme might not be going as successfully as planned, suggested a problem. When the news contained in the blog circulated, Tesco's shares dropped by 11.25p to 379p, wiping not far short of a billion pounds off the value of the company (albeit temporarily) and market traders attributed this to the blog.

The biggest challenge of all is the requirement to keep publishing. Media need content. The challenge to brands is the same as it is to conventional publishing: produce relevant and interesting content, regularly and ideally to a timetable that the audience can come to rely on. Brands will have to ask themselves the same questions that successful media organisations confront on a daily basis. Who is my audience? Where are they? What channels do I need to employ in order to reach them? What are they interested in? How can we engage them?

For some organisations the news that emerges from the activities within the business may provide sufficient content to engage the audience. For example, Whole Foods Market has demonstrated that it can create magazine content that is similar in quality and interest to conventional food publications. Electronic Arts occupies a space where intelligence on upcoming developments in gaming presented in a compelling way can compete with similar shows created by TV production companies and delivered by broadcasters. For other organisations, there simply isn't enough content emerging from their activities to sustain a compelling communications channel. This does not mean that the organisation cannot foster its own media outlet. It does, however, mean that, like the Australian beer brand, it may be better to act as a publisher of content created by others rather than relying solely on your own.

Rob Brown, FCIPR (@RobBrown) has worked in PR for 20 years and for a decade has held senior PR positions within major global advertising networks: Euro RSCG, McCann Erickson and TBWA. He is the author of *Public Relations and the Social Web* (2009), a board director at the CIPR 2010–2011 and founding chair of the CIPR Social Media Panel.

Chapter 14

Russell Goldsmith

Broadcast is changing as viewing habits shift online, but with more than 24 hours of video being uploaded to YouTube every minute, PRs face new challenges to achieve cut-through when using broadcast to engage directly with their audiences in social media.

Many communications professionals still judge the success of the broadcast element of their PR campaign on whether their brand's spokesperson was interviewed on BBC *Breakfast*'s sofa or the *Today* programme on BBC Radio 4. Yet, whilst TV and radio still provide a mass audience reach, the broadcast landscape has changed considerably over recent years and continues to do so, as more people receive their news from online and social media in particular.

Traditional broadcasters have recognised this fact themselves, offering audiences the opportunity to engage with their programmes via their websites, mobile apps, Twitter feeds and Facebook Pages. Similarly, previously print-only media owners can now arguably be defined as broadcasters, with newspaper and magazine websites carrying more video and audio content. The result is a huge opportunity for brands to secure broadcast coverage online as well as on air. However, it's within social media that the real breakthrough has occurred for organisations to engage directly with their audience, whether that is through the vast network of bloggers who have influence over their growing follower base, or though their own social network communities.

Making the leap from traditional to online broadcast coverage can be quite simple to achieve, as proved by McDonald's with its Menu Board Labelling campaign in 2011, aimed at gaining maximum exposure following the announcement of the Department of Health's 'Public Health Responsibility Deal'. In this instance, McDonald's, along with other fast food chains, aimed to comply with the initiative by putting the calorific value of each product it offered onto its menu boards.

To take ownership of the debate, McDonald's offered filming opportunities to broadcasters in one of its restaurants. Importantly, it also produced B-roll footage for the media, enabling it to control the visual and verbal messages being delivered on air. By being proactive in this manner, the story featured as the main news item on BBC *Breakfast*, ITV's *Daybreak* and across Sky News throughout the day. However, by spending just a couple of hours in an edit suite, a three-minute video news feature was also produced using the same B-roll footage that was then offered to all national newspaper websites. The result was a video report focusing specifically on how McDonald's was changing its menu boards, which ran on the websites of *The Express*[120], *The Times*, *The Independent*, *The Guardian*, *The Telegraph* and *The Sun*, extending the coverage way beyond traditional broadcast.

Becoming the media and content owner

A potentially more challenging online PR task for brands lies in how to generate positive conversation about them within social media outside of the current news agenda. This is where communications teams need to look at what broadcast media assets they have and work them harder through online networks.

Social media is about conversation, and when you consider topics that often 'trend' in the UK on Twitter, they are regularly based around traditional broadcast content, whether that be reality TV shows like ITV's *X Factor* or documentaries such as the BBC's *Frozen Planet*. What if a brand could create

---

[120] *Daily Express* Online, Emily Fox, McDonald's Labels Menus with Calorie Count, 6 September 2011: http://cipr.co/wm9DPp

its own live content that online viewers could share and comment on? If produced and distributed in the right targeted environments, then you don't necessarily need to be on national TV to achieve the same result, as proven by Vodafone McLaren Mercedes when launching the new livery of its car ahead of the 2011 F1 season. By providing F1 fans and bloggers exclusive access to the live stream of the event on its website and Facebook Pages, the excitement of the team's drivers Jenson Button and Lewis Hamilton unveiling the new car live online generated so much discussion on Twitter that it started to trend.

Video has been one of the biggest growth areas online, 34.2 million UK internet users watched 8.4 billion videos in January 2012 according to Comscore. It's therefore important to find the most effective use of video, appropriate to the target audience, to deliver the campaign message that the ROI will be judged on.

This is where interactive video, whether live or on-demand, can deliver positive results within social media. It provides an opportunity for the brand to be both content provider and media owner, allowing it to engage directly with its end audience. One way to achieve this is by producing a live and interactive Web TV show. A great example of a brand that did just that is Saga, in the lead up to the 2010 UK general election.

Saga, whose targeted audience is those aged over 50, saw an opportunity to position itself as the authoritative voice when it came to discussing issues affecting that particular demographic, such as pensions, healthcare and inheritance tax. It convinced each main party leader to take part in an interactive Web TV show where questions were submitted by the viewing audience online and via Twitter. Whilst the Labour leader and then Prime Minister Gordon Brown's[121] interview was pre-recorded inside 10 Downing Street, both the Conservative David Cameron[122] (from a conference centre) and Nick Clegg[123] of the LibDems (in a studio) faced a live online audience answering questions selected from thousands that had been submitted, due mainly to the fact that the show was featured on a host of national websites such as

---

[121]StudioTalk Saga Speaks to Gordon Brown: http://cipr.co/wLoYDI
[122]StudioTalk Saga Speaks to David Cameron: http://cipr.co/xoH4cy
[123]StudioTalk Saga Speaks to Nick Clegg: http://cipr.co/x76O1I

BBC News Online, *The Sun*[124] and *The Express*, as well as many sites targeted at the over-50s.

More brands have started to use Web TV to engage with their own communities by broadcasting live into the Timeline of their Facebook Pages. This means that anyone who has 'Liked' that Page will then be alerted to the live event in their own news feed and will be able to watch it without leaving their Facebook Page. They can share the broadcast feed with their friends, meaning they can watch it too without having previously 'Liked' the brand's Page but then, hopefully, will do so. This helps with the viral spread of the content and the brand's Page. Successful examples include Barclays, which has streamed live interviews with Premiership players into its Barclays Football Facebook Page. By becoming the broadcaster, this fan engagement programme helps maximise the brand's sponsorship of the sport.

Organisations can further promote Web TV shows by inviting their own customer base to watch the show, using HTML email alerts to create an appointment to view and encourage questions in advance and then again after the live event to come back and watch it on demand.

Proving ROI in social media

One of the hardest jobs PR has when it comes to social media, particularly on Facebook, is in proving the ROI of a campaign, especially when it's centred on viewing content with no direct call to action. For example, getting consumers to part with their cash through Facebook has proved a difficult task, even for established online retailers such as ASOS. International director, Jon Kamaluddin, said that the ASOS Facebook Store, which enabled its customers to purchase items without leaving the social network, was not delivering as well as expected.

If a brand as successful as ASOS is struggling to get people to spend through Facebook, what are the chances for the rest of us, especially when considering a study by Havas Media Social and Lightspeed Research in 2011,

---

[124]*The Sun*, Charlotte Brown, Saga Chats with Gordon Brown, 12 January 2011: http://cipr.co/xfROZh

which found that 89% of people had not bought anything via Facebook and 44% didn't have any interest in doing so?

One way that brands are starting to achieve this is by using interactive video player technologies such as LinkTo™, which enable viewers to click on hotspots within the video to either purchase product, opt-in for more information or, in the case of P&G's Febreze, print off a unique coupon to redeem in store.

P&G had previously used overlay technology, but the issue it had faced was that whilst viewers of interactive videos regularly engage by clicking on highlighted hotspots to get more information on particular products, if the product itself is a low-value ticket item, the consumer is less likely to add it into a shopping basket for a one-off purchase. This may work for exclusive promotions, as achieved by Heinz with its campaign allowing UK Facebook Fans to personalise a can of Heinz tomato soup to send to a friend who happened to be ill, but for a product that is part of your regular shopping list, there's not necessarily a need to buy it there and then.

By integrating LinkTo technology with a couponing system, so that when a viewer clicks on a hotspot in a video or when the video finishes, the video player automatically goes to an interactive page where the viewer can fill in a form and print off a unique coupon to redeem in store rather than online, P&G saw an instant response to its campaign. This launched on the Febreze Fabric Refresher brand's UK Facebook Page. Importantly, this also provided P&G with data collection and key insight into its customer database.

Blogger outreach and video SEO

Whilst national and targeted websites provide a large audience reach and Facebook is a popular destination for many campaigns, two other areas that can't be ignored when it comes to using video within social media include blogger engagement and video-sharing sites such as YouTube. Both of these can also become powerful tools in improving natural search results, proving that 'content is still king'! According to Forrester Research, you are 53 times more likely to appear on the front page of a Google search if your site contains video that is supported with keyword-tagged copy. Results for SEO can be improved even further by getting the public to share, comment on, embed and Tweet about your content, as Google provides results based on social search too. Twitter, in particular, has become a key driver in video traffic and so, if an influential blogger with lots of followers can embed a video on his/her blog and then Tweet the link, there's a stronger likelihood their followers will click through to view.

A recent example of an organisation that used all of these tools to good effect is heritage children's shoe brand Start-rite shoes. The company was keen to build a community around a series of instructional video guides it had produced such as 'how to fit children's shoes' but wanted it to be more than just about providing information one way and instead encourage feedback and a return path to purchase product too. It achieved this by building a custom channel on YouTube – www.youtube.com/startriteshoes – which enabled it to create a new vehicle for regular dialogue with parents, mums in particular, and build loyalty by broadcasting its own series of Web TV shows live, entitled 'Mum's Half Hour' through the social media platform every month and afterwards on demand. The key to the campaign was to recruit a panel of mums to be interviewed each week on subject matters close to their hearts and minds. As well as the content being offered to national media, including being featured in the TV listing of *The Independent*, each episode was offered to bloggers to embed on their pages as well as in Facebook and discuss on Twitter; crucially, key influential mummy bloggers were also invited onto the show. The mums panel played an integral role in the shaping of each show, feeding into the themes and content and advising on subjects and issues that mattered most to them. The resulting feedback from the mummy bloggers was extremely positive, with comments saying it was inspirational, giving mums the chance to share ideas and that there was enough content for the shows to be twice as long!

It's not just about video

It should be remembered that there is more to online broadcast than purely producing video content, and audio podcasts are a very popular route to reach an audience, particularly in the business-to-business space where there are limited opportunities to gain coverage on traditional broadcast. For example, there are many websites aimed at reaching small businesses that are keen to include rich media content, but will not necessarily have the time, resources or indeed budget to produce it. Offering those site editors editorially balanced audio features in the form of ready-made podcasts for them to include on their site makes their site more 'sticky' for their audience to come back and spend more time on. Those podcasts can also be uploaded to iTunes and, if updated regularly, listeners can then subscribe to the feed and have the content delivered directly to their iPods to listen to at home, in the office or on the move. The CIPR itself practises this exact method of distributing content with its own CIPR TV[125] series regularly featuring highly in the top management and marketing podcast charts on iTunes.

Finally, the charity Epilepsy Action took the concept of audio broadcast in social media one step further for its own awareness week when it created its own radio station that broadcast live through its Facebook Wall and website from 8am to 8pm, enabling the audience to call in to the live shows that were especially dedicated to dealing with epilepsy. The one-day online radio station proved so innovative and popular it was shortlisted for the best use of PR in the 2011 *PR Week* awards.

Social broadcast PR

This chapter started by looking at how PRs will need to achieve cut-through when using broadcast to engage directly with their audiences in social media. However, rather than being daunted by the challenge, it should instead be embraced and seen as a fantastic opportunity for brands. Social media are a digital advocacy platform used to share information. Broadcast has an ability to bring a story to life, as well as excite, enthuse and engage an audience. When you combine both tools, and remind yourself that you no longer are as reliant on the 'professional' journalist but instead can communicate directly with your audience through a brand's own community or with bloggers who

---

[125]CIPR TV: http://cipr.co/cipr-tv

are advocates of your products and services, the result for PR teams is very powerful and exciting.

Russell Goldsmith (@russgoldsmith) has been involved in online marketing since 1995 and is now digital and social media director at markettiers4dc, the UK's leading specialist broadcast communications agency with clients that include Kellogg's, Vodafone, McDonald's and Camelot. He also co-founded How To TV in 2008 and launched its interactive video technology LinkTo.tv in 2009. Russell sits on the CIPR Social Media Panel and is a regular presenter on CIPR TV.

Chapter 15

Adam Parker

In a social media driven world, the fundamentals of good media relations practice – relevance, authority, engagement and relationship – are more important than ever.

To date it has been understandably common to find that the PR (and/or the marketing) function within an organisation has been given the exclusive responsibility for social media listening and engagement. Increasingly, however, many organisations are realising that social media are unique communications tools that allow all parts of the organisation to engage in relevant conversations. This might be the customer service agent dealing with a complaint on Twitter or the sales executive following up a sales-specific question posed on a LinkedIn group. After all, PR people aren't the only ones allowed to use a telephone in an organisation, so why should they be the only ones using social media?

In such an environment, what is the role of the PR practitioner? The answer is they have a number of important roles to play in relation to social media. Arguably key among these currently is acting as a change consultant – advising, guiding and training the different parts of the organisation in effective and coherent social media engagement to ensure associated risks are managed and that there is consistency of approach. They also need to ensure that they are aware of wider conversations in social media as a whole so that they can respond to any reputation issues, internal or external, that may arise.

Roles such as these represent a return to the fundamentals of public relations, as social media have provided organisations with the means to converse efficiently and directly with more of their relevant publics.

Despite the social media revolution, the long-established media of print, TV, radio and more traditional online publishing still wield a vast amount of potential for influence and therefore media relations are also likely to remain a major element of a PR practitioner's responsibilities for some time yet. Given the blurring of media boundaries and the importance of key bloggers and other online content producers, perhaps *influencer* relations may be a more appropriate term these days.

The tactics and tools involved in influencer relations have remained largely unchanged for many years. Media lists of email and telephone contact details, either self-generated through research or purchased, have been used to facilitate telephone conversations, email correspondence and face-to-face briefings with varying degrees of success. Increasingly, however, interactions on Twitter are shaping some of the most important conversations relating to the media agenda as a whole. When it comes to media influencers, further evidence of Twitter's pre-eminence is the extent to which the media have embraced it. A recent survey[126] found that over 80% of journalists maintain a Twitter profile and the number one reason for doing so was so they could share their stories more widely.

No one is calling an end to the traditional elements of PR, however, and one suspects that a large proportion of influencer relations activity will continue to take place in the 'real' world for the foreseeable future. However, if you haven't integrated Twitter into your influencer relations approach, rather than just using it as a channel to communicate with your PR peers, you risk being left behind or, worse still, left out of key conversations.

So how do we translate influencer relations activities into the Twitter environment? What considerations should be applied, which tools should be used and which tactics employed?

---

[126]How Online Content Creators Use, Engage In, and Perceive Social Media: http://cipr.co/z30Sch

Identify

There are many ways to identify relevant media influencers on Twitter:

- *Get involved* – by being active on Twitter and becoming part of the community, by sharing information and engaging in discussions you will come across relevant individuals – journalists, editors, bloggers – who are likely to have voices in the wider media. The viral effect of Twitter and social media in general will help you discover the people most relevant to you.
- *Look up current contacts* – chances are you will have existing lists of media contacts who you already know. You can research these people specifically to discover which social media channels they are using themselves.
- *Search* – use free tools such as Twitter Search, Social Mention[127] and Followerwonk[128] to look for individuals on Twitter who are potentially relevant to you. You can also utilise directories which have been created for easy access to the right individuals. Some of these directories are paid-for services.
- *Curated lists* – sites like Listorious[129] and PeerIndex save you time with their lists of Twitter accounts that have already been curated into groups by other individuals.

Having identified relevant influencers on Twitter, there is then a question of whether you take account of any of the online tools that have appeared in recent months which claim to measure the influence of a particular person or account in social media. Two of the best known are Klout[130] and PeerIndex,[131] both of which have proprietary algorithms that use indicators such as frequency of Tweets, size of network, extent of re-Tweets and mentions by others to calculate an 'influence' score. However, influence, as any measurement expert will tell you, is about much more than just a number of re-Tweets.

---

[127]Social Mention: http://cipr.co/w62bwR
[128]Followerwonk: http://cipr.co/wAAcdw
[129]Listorious: http://cipr.co/wa6FlA
[130]Klout: http://cipr.co/zUiceN
[131]PeerIndex: http://cipr.co/yQN4mG

It requires work that is far beyond generic scoring and in simple terms is about measuring the extent to which actions you can observe have led to a different outcome for a given objective than would have been the case otherwise.

Despite the controversy in their methodology, used mindfully, measures such as these can still be useful. At the very least they do serve as an indicator of the extent to which a particular member of the Twitter community is likely to reach people with a message and provoke a reaction. It is probably fair to say, for instance, that if a person's account is rated low by such measures, say less than 20 in the case of Klout or PeerIndex, then the person in question is less likely to cause much in the way of ripples within Twitter itself. If only because such a low score often means the person in question doesn't actually Tweet very often in the first place. So even if you don't buy into these metrics as absolute measures of influence, they can often be useful from an initial triage point of view.

That is not to say that a person with such a score won't be influential. They could be a senior reporter for a major media outlet who just doesn't Tweet very often. For instance, Charles Bremner,[132] *The Times*'s correspondent in Paris, has a PeerIndex score of 11 at the time of writing (10 January 2012). This would imply that Mr Bremner is far less 'influential' than myself with a score of 42. This is clearly ridiculous if one is assessing the likelihood that Mr Bremner is potentially influential with regard to issues pertaining to France. In fact, Mr Bremner's score is probably low simply because he only Tweets very occasionally – three times since August 2011.

This demonstrates that in assessing the potential for someone to have influence, you must continue to look at things from a real world perspective and not be completely taken in by algorithmic social media metrics.

Listen

By now most organisations will have some sort of online monitoring system set up to alert them to relevant mentions of brands, products, topics and/or

---

[132]PeerIndex, Charles Bremner: http://cipr.co/yIRzwD

people when they occur on media outlets' websites. These services will generally also include similar mentions within social media communities.

The biggest issue with such listening platforms in a social media context is often that you are likely to get results that are relevant to different functions of the organisation and are not related to the influencers you have identified.

The simplest solution to this issue is to make sure you follow all the influencers you have identified on Twitter, and this is clearly an appropriate action anyway in order to allow you to engage with them (see below). However, there are still two challenges to overcome to achieve a curated listening solution.

Firstly it is difficult to keep track of the activity in your Twitter stream as a whole, particularly if you have different discrete groups of people you want to listen to. Secondly you are only aware of what they are saying if you are viewing your Twitter stream 24/7, which is highly impractical.

To solve the first difficulty to some extent, you can use a combination of Twitter lists and Twitter productivity tools like TweetDeck[133] or HootSuite[134]. For this example we will use TweetDeck.

Initially, create Twitter lists of discrete groups of Twitter accounts that you consider to be related in some way. Then use TweetDeck in order to view these streams side by side so you can follow each group more easily. You can then filter your columns within TweetDeck to search for specific keywords, meaning you can analyse your list of influencers quickly and efficiently by way of filtering. TweetDeck allows you to create multiple columns so you can categorise different groups of influencers.

To help with the second challenge you can use a service such as Twilert[135] to send you email alerts when someone mentions a specific term you have allocated. The downside of this is you will receive alerts whenever anyone on Twitter – as opposed to just your influencers – mentions the term you have allocated.

---

[133]TweetDeck: http://cipr.co/zQ8nrb
[134]HootSuite: http://cipr.co/xQ5OFD
[135]Twilert: http://cipr.co/Akq2qM

If your need for curated listening is significant, it may be worth investing in a paid solution to media influencer identification and listening.

Engage

Before considering influencer engagement on Twitter it is important to note that contact outside of social media is still likely to be the primary way you pitch stories to a journalist, for example, as the vast majority of them still prefer personalised email pitches where PR content is concerned.

The practicalities of engaging with media influencers on Twitter are mainly around its asynchronous nature. Having identified them you can then follow them, but it's unlikely they will follow you back. The evidence for this is that the vast majority of media influencers have a follower count that exceeds the number of accounts they follow with a ratio of between five to ten times greater being typical. In other words, if an influencer is following one hundred people, they often have between five hundred and a thousand followers.

If they don't follow you back this creates two key challenges for engagement. Firstly they won't see the Tweets you make and secondly you won't be able to send them a private direct message because doing so requires both accounts to be following each other.

This means that it is a necessity that you invest the time in trying to get to know the people who are important to you and seeking out opportunities to potentially engage them in conversation on Twitter by listening to them comprehensively.

Building a relationship within Twitter to the point where an influencer follows you back is itself often evidence that you have demonstrated your relevance and investment in that relationship. The ability to Direct Message someone that comes with this is to be prized, as this is still a far less used direct communication method than email, meaning that the likelihood of the influencer reading and taking notice of your message should be higher. However, use this function sparingly or you may just undo all the good work you did building up the relationship in the first place and you will probably find that the next time you try to Direct Message the person concerned, they have unfollowed you.

Conclusion

In a world where news often breaks on Twitter and the majority of media influencers are active in this community, many key conversations occur here. PR practitioners must therefore ensure that they have invested the time in identifying which significant media influencers to their organisation's objectives are among them, and ensure that they have the skills, knowledge and systems in place to effectively listen and potentially engage with them in this dynamic medium.

For those who do, it is an exciting, powerful and more interactive addition to their influencer relations activities. Those who don't, risk missing out on playing a role in important conversations that could shape their organisation's reputation.

Adam Parker (@AdParker) is chief executive of RealWire[136], an online press release distribution service that recently launched *Lissted*, a tool for discovering the media on Twitter. He is a chartered accountant and previously spent nine years with PwC in its audit, corporate finance and consulting practices. He blogs at www.showmenunumbers.com.

---

[136] RealWire: http://cipr.co/xBrkFC

Chapter 16

Julio Romo

For too long public relations has been seen solely as media relations – the discipline of engaging and promoting a client's viewpoint through the media. Much has been written about the media industry's demise because of the rise of social networking and associated channels. This belief could not be further from the truth.

New channels have emerged. Journalism, and the media landscape it inhabits, has changed. And new influencers have entered the fray. The skills needed for successful engagement, though, remain the same.

Having a core understanding of how the media works, audiences network and influencers behave is central to online media relations.

Through the pessimism about the death of journalism you see that this profession is adapting to how the audience works and consumes news. Publishers and journalists are changing how they work to ensure their content is relevant in the real-time world that we live in today.

Until the rise of digital and social channels, our engagement with the media was, for some PRs, through a hat-trick of activity – breakfasts with journalists, lunch with journalists and/or dinner with journalists. This tactic was, for established public relations practitioners, central to how coverage was secured for clients and employers.

The new influencers

The rise of the internet has changed how we consume news and content. The Web has empowered people, giving us the platform and opportunity to broadcast and share our thoughts and opinions with fellow enthusiasts. Bloggers and forum administrators are professionals in their own right. They bring together an audience that shares interests.

The UK's Chartered Institute of Public Relations (CIPR) describes PR as 'the discipline that looks after reputation – with the aim of earning understanding and support, and influencing opinion and behaviour.' The CIPR adds 'it is the planned and sustained effort to establish and maintain goodwill and mutual understanding between an organisation and its publics.'

This is a simple and effective way to describe the work of PR professionals. The description captures efficiently what the job of a PR entails – earning understanding and support, as well as establishing and maintaining goodwill and mutual understanding. What it does not focus on are the channels, allowing us the opportunity to engage with the audience through whatever medium is available.

Today, PRs can engage with the audience and the journalists, bloggers and forum administrators online in a transparent manner.

Understanding the role, behaviour and workflow of influencers is, like in traditional media relations, central to successful online media engagement.

Filled with contacts relevant to your sector is the address book, traditionally used for names, addresses and phone numbers. Perhaps it also had a record of the stories and dates that you pitched to your counterparts in the media.

Because of social networking, today you have a range of open channels through which you can engage with journalists and online influencers. Channels which should not be exclusive, but complementary to traditional media relations.

Open channels like Twitter provide PRs and communications professionals with the opportunity to follow their contacts and see, learn and listen to their daily life and routine.

While traditional media relations brought together PRs and journalists because of work, online engagement is also based on areas of mutual interest.

Pitching an idea or a story to a journalist is very different to pitching to a blogger or other online influencer. Too many PRs make the mistake of assuming that because bloggers carry content, they work like journalists. They don't.

Let's use the example of Burson-Marsteller US, which, in May 2011, decided to engage with influential blogger Chris Soghoian. Burson's Washington DC Media Practice Director, John Mercurio, reached out to Soghoian, offering him the opportunity to author 'an op-ed this week for a top-tier media outlet.' The approach was cold and written in a manner that highlighted the possible lack of a working relationship between the two parties.

Soghoian rebuffed Mercurio and made the email correspondence public,[137] leading to Facebook being outed as Burson's client.

The saga highlighted the importance of understanding how bloggers work and what motivates them. Having positive working relationships is as key to online media relations as it is to traditional engagement with journalists.

Before the pitch

Traditional and online commentators today have a presence on a range of social networks. For many, these networks are a source that adds value, comments and insight on breaking news stories.

Before pitching, establish yourself online and get to know the community that you wish to engage with. Remember, a cold approach is as useless online as it is through traditional channels.

You might find that journalists, bloggers and social media influencers are already following you. Create a network that is unique to the brands that you manage and invite influencers to join your community. Listening is central to understanding how you can shape the content and story that you wish to promote.

---

[137]Pastebin, Soghoian, Mercurio email correspondence: http://cipr.co/zjhHex

Media outlets like the UK's *Guardian*[138] and Sky News,[139] as well as international wires and outlets like The Associated Press[140] and Al-Jazeera[141] have open Twitter Lists listing the journalists and producers who are on Twitter. The *New York Times* goes a step further and dedicates a page of its website to listing the active journalists and newsroom accounts that are on Twitter.[142]

Creating a digital address book today could not be easier.

The story

Social networking has enabled brands and organisations to become storytellers. It has empowered people into sharing and reporting content. Brands have a wide range of channels at their disposal, enabling them to humanise their views and stories.

While you might have one story to tell, you have separate audiences to share it with. Each audience group has a network that is interested in both the story at large and the angle relevant to it's own community, which is why you should not spam all journalists with the same press release.

Segment the story to ensure that, as Simon Bowen from Bowen, Craggs & Co says, your audience and the individual media outlets 'have some sort of edge over their competition.'

Outreach and pitching your story

One of the downsides of having a presence on Twitter and other open networks, though, is that you will be competing with other communicators in

---

trying to secure the attention from journalists and other influencers. That said, when pitching, remember that journalists and social influencers use Twitter and other digital channels as a source for information, to scope out potential scoops and crowdsource case studies or insight for a story or blog that they are working on, creating proactive and reactive engagement opportunities.

Research in 2010 by Cision and The George Washington University revealed that content on social media channels 'is supplementing the research done by journalists.' While getting the story right will remain the primary focus, social media are providing additional content and insight and crunching the time between breaking news events going mainstream.

Journalists

Engage with journalists when you know that they might be checking their Tweets. For many outlets, across sectors – national, business and consumer – their newsrooms will have a structure that they will try to adhere to. As with traditional media relations, know the inner working of the titles that your journalist works for. When is morning conference? When do they have to file content by? What stories are they covering? When are they most active on Twitter? Are they always on call – do they take part in work Tweet conversations out of office hours? What are the times of the day when they are most active?

There are some key points to remember when reaching out to journalists and influencers online. While you can pitch through Twitter, remember the limitations of this platform – it is open and you have 140 characters for your pitch, picture, link or video. Twitter is a good starting point that works well to develop the relationships with journalists and influencers.

It is essential that your contacts get the part of the story that is relevant to them – segment the story and the content (video, interviews and images) accordingly.

The strength of Twitter is that you can and should Tweet directly to journalists, avoiding the mass-emailing exercise that has plagued public relations. One-to-one conversations enable the PR to better understand what each individual journalist requires, empowering the PR to customise the story for each journalist accordingly.

A journalist's working day is hectic, which is why they want efficiency in your approach. When emailing press releases, PDFs and Word documents can create a problem – internal mail systems can block content. Use the body of the email to send your story once they have signalled on Twitter that they are interested. Also, remember that email is no longer real-time, but a tool with which to get the extra content to journalists you have already pitched to on Twitter and other real-time platforms.

Bloggers

Like pitching to journalists, effective blogger outreach is always better if you have an understanding of what they write about and how long they have been blogging for. While for the majority of bloggers it's about personal interest, it can also be about securing professional recognition for themselves, a subject or cause. News outlets today might maintain blogs for their individual journalists, but blogger outreach is about reaching those that are independent from the media.

First and foremost, search and catalogue blogs that are relevant to your area of business. Make sure that you read them on a regular basis. Get to understand the blogger and associated contributors. Use Google, Technorati, AllTop and other similar databases. Media database Gorkana has recently joined the fray and added lists of bloggers to its own database, providing PRs who subscribe with details and background information on those who might cover their area of work.

Established technology blogger Robert Scoble[143] recently shared with his followers on Google+ an example of how Flipboard's developers reached out to him – a case of good blogger outreach.[144] The pitch was polite and had a

---

[143] Scobleizer: http://cipr.co/zevbry
[144] Google+, Robert Scoble profile: http://cipr.co/AxFdWd

link for the reason of the approach. The member of the team confirmed that he had been a follower and wanted to give him an opportunity to see a work in progress – the Flipboard iPad app.

Robert confirmed that the key points in Flipboard's successful pitch were: they got in early – the more time, the better your chance, allowing the blogger to provide feedback; they had done their research on him, his area of interest and how he worked; they focused on a 'hot area' – giving him an angle that he was interested in. Importantly, Flipboard kept the pitch short – the approach was by email, direct and to the point.

Forum administrators and influencers

Forums and the audiences that populate them can be central to any online media relations initiative. Forums are monitored and provide journalists and bloggers with quality insight and, as such, engagement with administrators can enable your final audience to get the information that you wish to promote.

As with approaches to journalists and bloggers, historical and ongoing participation in forums and engagement with their administrators is essential before a direct pitch. Remember that administrators are the gatekeepers to a network that shares a common area of interest.

Forums exist for many business, consumer, political and technological areas of interest. The audiences that gather here do so because it is a place where they can get information and advice on a range of subjects.

The rules of online media relations are simple. They are the rules of best practice public relations. It is about better understanding those with whom we work, their workflow and business, their interests, likes and dislikes. Online and social media relations can improve how our stories and experiences get shared and reported.

Effective understanding of people will ensure that being good at public relations is no longer to be expected. Being great at understanding people will be the minimum prerequisite.

Julio Romo MCIPR [@twofourseven] is an independent communications consultant and digital strategist with over 14 years' experience working on global and local initiatives across a range of sectors. Today, he operates in Europe, the Middle East and Asia. Current and past clients include The Council of Europe, Du Mobile, Saudi Arabia's Ministry of Health, Abu Dhabi Tourism, Astro All Asia Network, BP Indonesia, Zanerva and Etiqa Insurance.

Part V

Monitoring and Measurement

Chapter 17

REAL-TIME PUBLIC RELATIONS

Philip Sheldrake

Real-time communication impacts public relations in ways that cannot be described simply as 'same as before but faster'! It is both a central cause and effect of what it means to practise PR in the digital age.

Twitter's rapid growth sparked the PR profession's interest in the so-called 'real-time Web'. In 2009, the advent of the real-time Web extended beyond Twitter when Microsoft's Bing, and then Google, launched real-time search, albeit leaning largely on Twitter contributions – Tweets. At the time of writing, Bing serves up real-time search results at http://bing.com/social[145] and Google has retired its early foray accessed via its 'Updates' feature, refocusing instead on the real-time Google+ social network.

Real-time communication impacts public relations in ways that cannot be described simply as 'same as before but faster'! Real-time communication pushes public relations practitioners towards the Excellence model of public relations, and raises the criticality of the discipline in every organisation.

What do we actually need to do in real-time?

Media monitoring has been around for decades of course. Public relations practitioners push press releases and sell-in case studies to journalists and bloggers, and a media monitoring company is retained to keep its eyes peeled for resultant coverage – and for unprompted coverage of course. A copy of coverage is made available to the PR team as and when, and complimentary coverage is celebrated.

---

[145]Bing Social: http://cipr.co/AdVEsM

Such monitoring services have increased their drumbeat over the years. The monthly report became weekly, and the weekly envelope gave way to the daily uploads to a Web service. But the emphasis remained one of monitoring, which The *Oxford English Dictionary* defines as:

> Monitoring: observe and check the progress or quality of (something) over a period of time; keep under systematic review; listen to and report on.

You can see that the definition is very much reflective, and anyone who has worked in public relations for more than a few years will know how these clippings are typically processed – slowly, reflectively. Today, it remains not too uncommon to see the primary interest in the clippings coming in the form of updating the coverage book in reception.

Any coverage demanding further action will be raised in the next team meeting, but media monitoring, as we've known it, feels viscerally separate from the day-to-day, hour-to-hour reality. It's almost more of an echo of what one did yesterday or a week ago or longer.

The thing about the real-time Web, however, is simply that it means your customers, indeed all stakeholders, are having conversations at the speed of…well…er…a conversation. The idea that a dialogue plays out in the Letters to the Editor pages over days and weeks turns out to have been little more than a temporary historical aberration. Conversations play out second by second, minute by minute on Twitter, blogs, forums, Facebook, Google+, Quora, on the talk pages of Wikipedia, on comment-enabled websites run by established news media from the BBC to CNN, from the *Financial Times* to the Huffington Post, and probably other shiny new services that have sprung up since the time of writing. And this has two major ramifications, meaning that monitoring alone is insufficient:

1. Your stakeholders' expectations of your participation in the real-time conversation may well have changed. Do you understand that? How have they changed? What does it mean to your organisation?

2. You also have to make the decision about which conversations you wish to enter in real-time before they're effectively over, or indeed before the conversation has run away with itself in the absence of moderating information and responses from you.

In other words, we're talking here about real-time communication, not just monitoring.

Complexity

Let's take a look at how this reality manifests itself in the day of a PR consultant: one who's living the dream in 1991, and one who's teetering on the edge in 2012. Complexity doesn't feature in 1991; everything is quite manageable, thank you. By 2012, however, things have become quite complicated indeed.

We're in 1991 and your campaign execution demands a vanilla media relations outreach. You need to contact 20 journalists across your target publications and broadcast media – your tier 1. You might also want to 'spray' the rest with a wire distribution. Effectively, then, you have 21 points of focus. A few of the target journalists are freelance and write for two or three key publications, and as you expect a bit of syndication, you have approximately three-dozen media to track.

Your clippings service sweeps up the coverage for you. The campaign results in coverage across the target media and wider afield, requiring assessment of sentiment (positive/neutral/negative) and readership. A share of voice analysis reviews all coverage in your 30-odd tier 1 media, and teases out the mentions of your brand, your product and those of your nearest competitors.

This is simple stuff. There are no mathematical products here, just some simple high school arithmetic based on averages and spreads. You may get in touch with one or two journalists if you feel that they might not have grasped the issue quite the way you think it should have been grasped, or perhaps you'll just make a note to address this the next time you catch up with them.

Now let's go back to the future, to today. Communication and media technologies proliferate and company-to-customer communication now competes for attention with customer-to-customer communication. Active and passive customer-to-customer and customer-to-company communication is multi-channelled and in the public domain. The format of communication has expanded massively beyond the press release to include blog posts, podcasts, video, Twitter, games, live Web chats, etc. Your customers don't distinguish between public relations and customer service, so neither can you.

This means that you now have many different ways and channels to engage with customers and prospects, and they have many ways to engage with you and each other. You employ continuous, active monitoring, and you're effectively involved in thousands – possibly millions – of relationships. In real time!

Where should I listen and how should I make sense of it, and what demands a response and what should I say and when should I say it, and to whom should I say it and where should I say it, and in which format should I say it? When you multiply these possibilities together, it becomes immediately clear that you're trying to deal with massive complexity, at least relative to your colleague from 1991. We have many more permutations and complexity than any human can juggle independently in a meaningful way.

Sometimes it's difficult to put this complexity into words, so I teamed up with a talented illustrator to paint the picture as of January 2011. We estimate the result has been viewed over a hundred thousand times, so you might like it too.[146]

Reality

Being the eyes, ears and mouth of an organisation to the drumbeat of the monthly, weekly and daily news was never easy.

Being the eyes, ears and mouth, with heightened sensitivity to influencing and being influenced in real-time, requires enhanced levels of strategic diligence, meticulous planning, training, constant attention to detail and rigorous measurement.

'Perception is reality' was a common axiom for marketing and public relations in the 20th century. However, the advent of the real-time social Web brings an unprecedented and radical transparency, and in a relatively short time the situation has flipped to one of 'reality is perception'.

In the simplest terms, it's impossible to fake it. There's a reason why instances of people leading double lives are few and far between – it's incred-

---

[146]http://cipr.co/JTCAFb

ibly hard work to maintain the façade day in and day out. Given the radical transparency enabled by social media, pretending to be something you're not or, perhaps more kindly, attempting to project an image that isn't entirely reflective of reality, cannot be sustained in real-time for long; especially so when you have many people from all parts of the organisation participating in these conversations.

In other words, PR can only be authentic – defined as having the quality of an emotionally appropriate, significant purpose and responsible mode of human life. The real-time social Web leads us, then, to the Excellence model of public relations: Grunig's fourth model of two-way, symmetric communication fostering mutually beneficial relationships between an organisation and its publics.

What does success look like?

As required and guided by your public relations strategy, success in real-time public relations demands answers to the following questions:

- *What?* – active listening; responding with the appropriate content, information and insight; creating proactive opportunities to converse with stakeholders in real time; feeding acquired knowledge into the organisation in real-time.
- *Who?* – the right member of your team enters the conversation, determined by constituent expectations, consistency, topic, expertise, availability, time zone and language.
- *How?* – adopting an appropriate tone of voice and appropriate content format; employing the agreed system for workflow management; understanding how and when to escalate.
- *When?* – as timely as the conversation demands (often minutes or hours).

The essentials

Real-time PR success requires:

- (re)connecting PR to the business;
- investment in knowledge, skills and policies;

- defined analytics and workflow;
- an appropriate culture;
- rigorous measurement and evaluation.

The very essence of real-time PR demands more than ever that we get back to basics and connect PR activity to the business needs, unambiguously, visibly, transparently, efficiently and relentlessly. This connection demands rigorous business management, effective internal communications and training. It demands the bold and bright articulation of your organisation's mission, vision and values, and a cascade down to the coalface that each and every employee understands and internalises.

The Cascade

Mission – why do we exist?
⇓
Values – what guides our behaviour?
⇓
Vision – what do we want to be?
⇓
Business objectives – to get from A to B
⇓
Strategy – the plan to get us from A to B
⇓
Strategic objectives – wholly necessary and sufficient to execute the plan
⇓
Tactics – activities to achieve the strategic objectives
⇓
Measurement and analysis – are we making progress in executing the strategy, and does the strategy remain valid?

Organisations that pay closer attention to the cascade (i.e. practise effective business performance management) will find the transition to real-time public relations easier than those that do not. The latter will have to deal with more fear, doubt, confusion, paralysis, inconsistency, lack of authenticity, missed opportunities and reputational risk.

Knowledge, skills and policies

Your team needs an updated appreciation of PR best practice. They need to be connected personally to the cascade, having a deep insight into your organisation's mission, values and vision, and how they inform and guide what they do and how they behave every single day. They need to be apprised of the demands of real-time PR.

You'll be looking to develop or draft in new skills: analytical capabilities, social media expertise (in the organisational, rather than personal, context), process design capabilities, quality assurance and audit expertise, tool procurement and interdisciplinary understanding (of related marketing, digital and customer service disciplines).

To assist everyone in this transition, you'll be looking to create, update or ratify PR and social media policy and guidance on tone of voice, customer care and the PR escalation process.

Analytics and workflow

Social analytics is about identifying, tracking, listening to and participating in the distributed conversations about a particular brand, product or issue, with emphasis on quantifying the trend in each conversation's sentiment and influence.

You'll need social analytics tools appropriate to your needs, fluency in their application, integration with other analytic capabilities (e.g. CRM) and fit for integration with your approach to business performance management.

You'll need to develop the workflow (aka process design), potentially with your social analytics service provider. You'll be looking to build quality into the process rather than just test for it. You'll review the integration of PR activity with related marketing and customer service activity, and provide appropriate training courses and reference documentation.

There have been many references to the workflow developed by the United States Air Force, and for good reason. You may find it a useful example.[147]

Culture

I consider the following cultural traits to be more suited to real-time public relations than otherwise. It will be for you and your leadership team to decide where and how your current culture may need adaptation.

1. Organisation-wide, influence-focused culture (appreciative of how influence goes around and comes around).
2. A culture built on team and personal goal alignment.
3. A culture that recognises there's potential influence in everything it does (and indeed what it might choose not to do).
4. A quality (TQM) focus.
5. A culture of customer focus.
6. A culture of innovation and continuous improvement.
7. A culture of social awareness and responsibility.

Measurement and evaluation

Chapter 19 addresses measurement and evaluation, so I won't add anything here other than to say that rigorous, continuous measurement and evaluation must be part and parcel of real-time PR.

It will be obvious by now that a lot of work goes into getting ready for real-time PR. On that basis alone, I recommend you start right now while you

---

[147]Wikipedia, US Air Force Web Posting Response Assessment: http://cipr.co/yJ4aHJ

can do so proactively; else you'll be forced to get real-time sooner or later, reactively, and probably in a fit of panic.

Good luck.

Philip Sheldrake (@sheldrake) is the author of *The Business of Influence: Reframing Marketing and PR for the Digital Age* (Wiley, 2011) and the Digital Marketing chapter of the CIM's book, *The Marketing Century*. He is a Chartered Engineer, Member of the CIPR, Founding Partner of Meanwhile, Founding Partner of Influence Crowd, Main Board Director of Intellect and Board Director of 6UK. He built and sold an award-winning PR consultancy. Philip co-founded the CIPR Social Media Panel and the CIPR Social Summer series; he chairs the CIPR's measurement and evaluation group and co-hosts CIPR TV. He blogs at philipsheldrake.com.

Chapter 18

Andrew Smith

It would be hard to find anyone who would argue that there is no value in listening to what stakeholders say about an individual, an organisation or an institution. Given that there appears to be such a universal consensus about its value, why does it continue to be a subject that divides opinion across the board?

Listening to your audiences has become a truism in both public and private sectors. And the concept is hardly new. Long ago and far away, businesses and organisations would send researchers out with a clipboard and survey to knock on doors and assail people in the streets to ask them their opinions.

However, for many decades, the techniques involved remained largely unchanged. Pollsters may have taken to calling people on the phone, and with the rise of the internet, the use of email and Web surveys ostensibly brought down the potential cost and reach of such exercises. But at root, this was still largely a case of surveying random samples of an audience in order to better understand what it was thinking and feeling – and to use this to anticipate how best to meet its needs – or, in a PR context, determine what messaging strategy and tactical activity to develop.

The use of market research and opinion poll data has been grist to the PR mill for some time – having said that, there have always been a number of caveats in its use. The old shoemakers' maxim comes to mind: fast, quality and cheap – but not all three at once. Clearly, the bigger the survey, the higher the cost involved – and typically the longer it would take to gather the data. Quick dipstick surveys may provide fast results, but the quality and depth would obviously be lacking. How much store would any organisation lay by such insight?

Not only this, but there was always the nagging doubt that those being surveyed were giving the pollster what they wanted to hear rather than what they honestly thought. Or rather, there was a potential disconnect between what people said and what they did.

What has changed in the last five years is the inexorable rise of social media. From the standpoint of the public, they now have an easy means of expressing their views and opinions about pretty much anything. Brands and institutions make for natural conversation fodder.

Conversely, organisations now potentially have immediate real-time insight into the thoughts, views and feelings of their stakeholder audiences in a way that would have been unthinkable in earlier times – not just customers, but journalists, politicians and other important influencers. And, in many cases, this comes at a trivial cost.

In light of which, the case for social media monitoring would appear self evident. What organisation would not want to listen to its audiences to determine what they think and feel about them? Happier customers tend to be more predisposed to buying a company's products, or voting for a political party. On the other hand, negative sentiment is a big red warning flag that says something is amiss and needs fixing.

However, given the almost universal agreement that social media monitoring is a good thing, what are the key challenges facing PR practitioners in harnessing the power of social media monitoring to better inform communication strategies and campaigns?

Perversely, one of the main issues is the sheer volume of data freely available. Whereas in the past, high quality real-time data was only available at great cost (if at all), pretty much anyone can create a low-cost social media monitoring dashboard with a tool like TweetDeck – for nothing. But anyone who has spent any time trying to monitor all but the most esoteric Twitter conversations will soon become numb to the torrent of Tweets cascading down a TweetDeck column – let alone being able to interpret what is being said and using this as the basis for action.

Even assuming that an organisation is able keep on top of what is being said, it raises a number of vital questions about resourcing and responsibilities. If a customer makes a complaint on Twitter, who should respond to it?

Should it be responded to in a public environment? Are some people's opinions more important than others? How much resource should an organisation allocate to monitoring social media and who should be responsible for it?

To give an example, BT (one of the world's leading communications services companies operating in over 170 countries) has a team of more than 30 full-time employees dedicated to monitoring what is being said about BT online (including on social media). And they are empowered to react and respond. Interestingly, this team falls under the remit of customer service rather than PR. Clearly, an organisation the size of BT has its own business objectives and challenges – but it is a useful example of the kind of issues and challenges that any organisation will face when attempting to determine the level of investment in social media monitoring.

Sentiment analysis

The rise in interest in social media monitoring has seen a commensurate rise in technology solutions available to meet this demand – solutions ranging from the free to the very costly. Perhaps the most interesting area is in the use of so-called automated sentiment analysis.

What is sentiment analysis? Quite simply, it is the attempt to deduce how somebody feels about a particular person, topic, issue or organisation based on what they say. Given the sheer volume of social media content available, technologies have emerged that attempt to automate this process of analysis. They fall into two broad camps. The first makes use of simple word matching based on dictionaries (or bags of words as some cynics describe them). Lists of 'positive' and 'negative' words are drawn up in advance, and any piece of content is then analysed and matched against these lists. If the balance of negative to positive words is higher, then the content is deemed 'negative' towards the subject.

The benefits of this kind of approach are that automated sentiment analysis tools can be created at low cost for the end user. Indeed, some tools such as Social Mention[148] are free to use. The downside is clearly accuracy. Critics

---

[148]Social Mention: http://cipr.co/wɪJIoF

of the 'bag of words' approach rightly argue that this technique can't deal with irony, sarcasm or slang – and thus the prevalence of so-called 'false positives' can be high, thereby adding to the resource overhead required to check the accuracy of the analysis. Having said that, there is no question that free tools such as Social Mention allow any organisation to at least test the concept of sentiment analysis in the context of social media for no monetary outlay, and can give them some idea as to what level of investment may be appropriate for them in the future. Low-cost tools such as UberVu[149] will also give the end user the ability to easily amend the sentiment rating if inaccurate assessments are spotted.

Contextual analysis

The opposing camp uses sophisticated computer algorithms and semantic analysis to provide a higher level of accuracy and refinement. These more contextually based tools allow for more accurate analysis of far higher volumes of content as well as being able to isolate sentiment from different viewpoints (big bankers' bonuses may be perceived negatively by the public and media. However, a banker who is going to receive a big bonus may see this differently). The only downside with this approach is clearly the comparatively high cost of such solutions, which will make them viable only for the very biggest of organisations (although that may change over time as usage rises and providers are able to offer these capabilities to a broader market for lower cost).

In tandem with the rise of automated sentiment analysis has been the introduction of influence rating services such as Klout,[150] PeerIndex[151] and PeopleBrowsr.[152] These tools have the potential to answer one of the other key challenges of social media monitoring – namely, if some people's views and opinions are more important than others (or perhaps need responding

---

[149]UberVu Login Page: http://cipr.co/w9Yut5
[150]Klout: http://cipr.co/zUiceN
[151]PeerIndex: http://cipr.co/yQN4mG
[152]PeopleBrowsr: http://cipr.co/yhvvOi

to more urgently than others), how do you identify who those people are? A tool such as PeerIndex, for example, will attempt to analyse an individual's online influence and then provide an overall score relative to a particular subject or topic. Using this kind of analysis could help PRs to determine whether someone who is voicing a negative opinion needs to be dealt with in a particular time-frame or in a certain way based upon their potential impact on a key stakeholder audience (although caveats clearly apply given the level of maturity of the technology).

Network topology

The other emerging aspect of social media monitoring is the concept of relationship network analysis. PR (and marketing generally) has traditionally been a very linear process. On a simplistic level, an audience is identified, a list of relevant journalists and media titles is built and content is fired at them with the hope that key messages will stick and influence the target audience. This approach ignores the interconnectedness of an internet-mediated world. To be fair, the means to actually track, measure and understand the nature of networked relationships has never really existed until recently. And network science has traditionally focused on technology rather than people. The pioneering work of people such as sociologist Nicholas Christakis[153] demonstrates the power and value of understanding network topology – whether of a computer network or a cadre of political bloggers. The marrying of social media monitoring with sentiment analysis, influence ranking and network analysis gives a glimpse of the opportunity for the PR profession.

In summary, it is hard to argue against using some form of social media monitoring – especially in the context of helping to guide and inform the development and execution of PR and communications programmes. Given the ability to test out approaches to social media monitoring at next to no cost, there seems no excuse for not trying it. Conversations about your organisation or brand are taking place whether you like it or not. Paying no attention to

[153]Amazon, Connected: The Amazing Power of Social Networks and How They Shape Our Lives: http://cipr.co/yA51hO

this conversation at all could be seen as negligent business practice in the modern world. The bigger challenges lie, though, in terms of how companies determine their level of investment and commitment to social media – and who should take responsibility for owning and managing those approaches. PR professionals should and must be involved in that debate. However, in order to win the battle, they must arm themselves with direct knowledge and understanding of the value of social media. Social media monitoring is a vital first step.

Andrew Smith (@andismit) is managing director of Escherman, a specialist online PR, SEO and analytics consultancy. Smith has been a consistent PR innovator, being among the first UK practitioners to exploit email (1991), the World Wide Web (1994) and Twitter (2007). Described as the 'de facto godfather of PR blogging', he is a regular speaker and media commentator on the integration of PR with social media, search optimisation and analytics.

Chapter 19

Richard Bagnall

Social media appear to be a measurement fanatic's dream. Finally we have a form of communication that appears easy to monitor and, via the digital breadcrumb trail that it leaves, easy to measure. However, not all is as it seems. The rise of software vendors automating vast swathes of content analysis into a one-size-fits-all platform leaves the PR industry facing very real problems. What's it to do – measure what is easy to capture but largely irrelevant or focus on measuring what matters? And how best to do that?

It used to be so simple. For years the pace of change in the media measurement industry reflected the pace of change in PR itself – pretty glacial. As an industry, media analysis and evaluation started to become more widespread in the late 1980s and early 1990s.

Back in those days my colleagues and I used to receive literally sack loads of paper clippings each day that would be sent to us either directly by our clients or from the press cuttings agencies. Clips would arrive days and often weeks after publication. The usual turnaround period that the evaluation agencies would work to was then a further two weeks as we read and analysed the clips according to each client's brief. Written reports would often arrive back with the clients weeks after the content had been published.

All of the evaluation companies tended to measure similar things. Categories would include the size of the article, its position in the paper and on the page, whether it included a headline (and if so the size of that), a photo, the article's tone, brand mentions, organisational and industry issues, inclusion of positive or negative messages, the media type and publication, the date, the journalist, whether spokespeople were included, the readership figure and frequently Advertising Value Equivalents (widely known in the industry as AVEs) and other things too.

The only way we differed from each other was in the amount and quality of the supporting written text and our approach to how we reported on the above categories. Many companies looked for unique angles with their own proprietary scoring systems where they factored different elements from the aforementioned categories with a weighting system to come up with their own magic formula number. And the vast majority of evaluation programmes concentrated on measuring purely the outputs (like newspaper clips) rather than the out-takes (what the target audience now thinks) or the outcomes (what they now may have done). Of course, newspaper clippings alone could only answer this part of the equation.

The side-effect of this disparate approach by the industry was that clients would often be confused, and the majority of the metrics themselves did not speak the language of the boardroom.

Progress

As the years passed, media evaluation became more mainstream around the world, and the differing methods of analysing the content spread. Then, in 2009, great progress was made when AMEC (the International Association for the Measurement and Evaluation of Communication), working in partnership with other global PR bodies, declared the Barcelona Principles, which were widely accepted. These were seven statements detailing how PR measurement could and should be done as best practice.

The seven principles are:

1. Goal setting and measurement are fundamental aspects of any PR programmes.
2. Measuring the effect on outcomes is preferred to measuring outputs.
3. The effect on business results can and should be measured where possible.

4. Media measurement requires quantity and quality.

5. AVEs are not the value of public relations.

6. Social media can and should be measured.

7. Transparency and replicability are paramount to sound measurement.

To lead the way, AMEC published its Valid Metrics Framework.[154]

The Valid Metrics Framework provides a template (shown below) whereby each communication tactic can be measured down the marketing funnel from awareness to knowledge and understanding, interest and consideration, support and preference and finally to action. The above-referenced Valid Metrics Framework document provides full details on how to use it.

It appeared that we were enjoying a new era in the PR and measurement industry – one where the industry had agreed to turn away from spurious

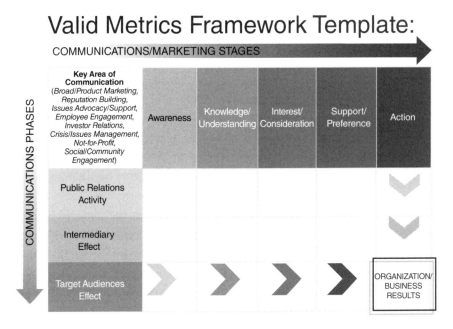

Source: AMEC Valid Metrics Framework

---

[154]AMEC, Barcelona Principles Valid Metrics Framework: http://cipr.co/KlpT7v

scores and weighted outputs and to focus on measuring outcomes based on objectives of campaigns. But something else had been changing.

Throughout the 'noughties', and with increasing urgency since 2005 with the early case studies of the potential crises to which companies were now exposed, online and social media were growing in popularity and importance. While organisations were working out what it all meant, whether it mattered, how to engage with the channel, and, if so, which department should be involved, new companies like Radian6, Sysomos and Brandwatch were being set up with the purpose of monitoring all of this new content (social media monitoring was covered in more detail in Chapter 18).

Back to the Dark Ages?

Quickly they realised that purely monitoring the content was not going to be enough and that they needed to analyse and attempt to bring meaning to the information as well. As these services have a one-size-fits-all approach, they began inventing scores and systems to measure content as if the previous 20 years hadn't existed. Worse, with the one-size-fits-all approach, all metrics had to be the same for all organisations regardless of each one's differing objectives, goals and tactics.

To cope with the vast volumes of content, it was apparent that humans couldn't analyse the content fast enough or cheaply enough, so automated algorithms using natural language processing (NLP[155]) techniques were deployed to analyse topics and tone in real time.

Other automated scores also started to be added as the industry tried to understand this new medium. It became increasingly apparent that influence spreads differently across social media than for mainstream media. No longer were communicators dealing with individual channels delivering their own unique audiences; now it was an interconnected channel offering multiple audiences – and each member of each of these audiences had their own audience. Although the vast majority of consumers may just observe, or lurk, there were some that seemed able to make things happen – whether accidentally

---

[155]Wikipedia, Natural Language Processing: http://cipr.co/x3aLrg

or in a more deliberate manner. These types of people came to be known as influencers. From a PR point of view, if they could be identified and targeted, the potential power to a brand would surely be significant.

The automated tools, of which there were more than 200 at all price levels by 2012,[156] rushed to come up with ways to identify these influencers using automated scoring and weighting systems. The best known of these new tools that focuses on influence is probably Klout, which calls itself 'The Standard of Influence'. But, as Philip Sheldrake, author of *The Business of Influence*[157] argues, true influence cannot be measured with a score. According to Sheldrake,[158] influence has been exerted when someone thinks something they wouldn't otherwise have thought or does something that they wouldn't otherwise have done.

As he says:

> 'What influence is not . . . Influence is definitely not some quantity invented by a PR firm, analytics provider, or measurement and evaluation company that rolls up a number of indices and measures into some relatively arbitrary compound formula that makes any appreciation of the underlying approach, variables and mathematics completely opaque to the end-user, thereby radically attenuating any little use it may have been but in such a way that it can be branded nicely and sold as "unique".'

Sheldrake develops his thoughts on understanding social media influence further in his book.

The similarities with the early media influence indexes and scores of so many traditional media analysis companies is striking.

The problems with the measurement and analysis of social media didn't stop here though: my own company, Metrica, trialled three of the best-known social media monitoring companies to see how they stacked up against each other. We set each company the same brief. We were looking

---

[156]Social Media Analysis, Directory of Companies: http://cipr.co/wz8Wx1
[157]*The Business of Influence*: http://cipr.co/Ase9gC
[158]SlideShare, Influence. The bullshit, best practice and promise: http://cipr.co/wLvAke

for English-language content only based around a tightly defined search string to do with a well-known IT company. We set them the same time period of two weeks and set up feeds direct from their databases to our own where we then pored over the results. To check the automated analysis, we had three expert analysts check the sentiment analysis that the automated systems had decreed for 500 posts each. We were shocked by the results. Some of the startling facts we discovered included:

- The total numbers of posts returned ranged from 281,000 found by one provider to 451,000 found by another. Some of the providers found the same piece of content repeatedly but counted it many times, failing to deduplicate effectively.
- At least one-third of the content found by each provider was not relevant to the brief that we had set them.
- Only 20% of the total content was found by all three of the providers on test.
- All three providers varied wildly in their ability to find content in the differing social media channels.
- The speed that they returned results also varied dramatically. One company averaged over 24 hours to return the content.
- The accuracy of their sentiment analysis was at best correct 61% of the time and at worst only 29% of the time.

These sorts of results are not unique to Metrica's research; many other companies have looked into the monitoring platforms and found similar results.

The unsuitability of automated systems for measuring social media in a meaningful manner has meant that there is now a concerted drive to look at setting standards and best practice.

AMEC, having succeeded previously driving the PR industry forward in its approach to measurement with the Barcelona Principles, is looking to repeat its success with a similar strategy. The organisation has set up a social media measurement standards group working in a coalition with global PR trade bodies that include the Institute for Public Relations, the Council of Public Relations Firms (both US trade associations) and in collaboration with the CIPR and PRCA too. The CIPR has already made great progress, with its research, measurement and planning toolkit updated to include an approach to measuring social media.[159]

AMEC has now assembled a team of experts representing companies from across the world to help drive the standards.

Areas of confusion identified by AMEC that will benefit from further clarity include:

- *Influence* – is there a best practice way to identify who has got it?
- *Sentiment* – has your content been analysed by man or machine? Do you know what error rate your approach should expect?
- *Engagement* – what constitutes engagement? Just because someone has clicked on a Facebook 'Like' button, does this mean that they engaged with your organisation or brand?
- *Monitoring/content* – what methods have you used to source your content, how fast is the company that you are using at retrieving data, how broad are its searches? Within the content returned, what amount should you expect to be relevant or spam or even porn?
- *Demographics/target audiences* – is there a way to bring target audience information into the reporting?

Interestingly, as marketers got used to the concept of paid media, owned media and earned media, it became apparent that the PR industry was not the only marketing discipline looking to establish standards. In October 2011, the first Social Media Measurement Standards Conclave[160] was held, which saw a coming together of a number of different trade bodies from across marketing to identify areas of potential collaboration and overlap. In addition to AMEC, IPR, CPRF and the CIPR, SNCR, Web Analytics Association, IABC and WOMMA were all represented. The Conclave largely agreed with AMEC on the key areas, although with a slightly different emphasis, and is currently focusing its work on:

---

[159]CIPR, Social Media Measurement: http://cipr.co/sm-measurement
[160]The Measurement Standard, The State of Setting Social Media Measurement Standards: http://cipr.co/xfweiG

1. Reach and engagement.
2. Influence and relevance.
3. Value/impact.
4. Content definition.
5. Sentiment and advocacy.

This is all still a work in progress and the results will not be available until after this book's publication, but it seems clear where the work is likely to take us. As with the Barcelona Principles, there won't be one number which will work across all social media measurement. Nor will there be one approach which will definitely be the right one. I'd expect to see, as one attendee at the Conclave put it, a GAAP (Generally Accepted Accountancy Principle) approach. I expect the standards to be guidelines rather than prescriptive techniques and a similar framework approach as the Barcelona Principles to be endorsed at AMEC's 2012 summit in Dublin in June.[161]

Practical next steps

Measuring social media can sound overwhelmingly complex. When confronted with a new-to-many channel and with so much content, flowing in real time, it can be tempting to settle for accepting metrics that come included with monitoring platforms. My advice is: don't.

When looking to analyse your coverage, think as you have always been trained to think. Stop and ask yourself what your objectives are. Make sure that you tailor your metrics back around these objectives. Every time that you feel you have a potential metric, ask yourself why is this relevant/so what? Do this two or three times per metric before you accept it. If it doesn't pass the 'so what' factor, it shouldn't make it in to your analytics.

Until AMEC, the Coalition and attendees of the Conclave publish the next steps, I would recommend following Don Bartholomew's approach. Don blogs regularly and is one of the brains at the forefront of the measurement industry.

---

[161]AMEC, Dublin to host 2012 European Summit: http://cipr.co/wNmfTn

Don has adapted the marketing funnel and suggests it should now read:

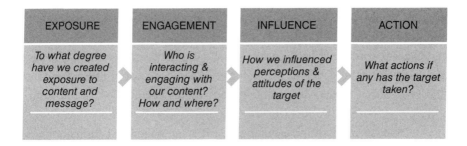

EXPOSURE	ENGAGEMENT	INFLUENCE	ACTION
To what degree have we created exposure to content and message?	Who is interacting & engaging with our content? How and where?	How we influenced perceptions & attitudes of the target	What actions if any has the target taken?

He also believes that a framework approach is the right one. Below we can see how he suggests appropriate metrics for each of the steps of the funnel and against each of the integrated types of media.

INTEGRATED MEASUREMENT - PESO

FLEISHMAN INTERNATIONAL COMMUNICATIONS HILLARD

	EXPOSURE	ENGAGEMENT	INFLUENCE	ACTION
Paid	• Opportunities to see • Impressions • Click-thrus • CPM • TRPs	• Interaction rate • Durationg (time spent) • Branded search • Cost per click	• Purchase consideration • Change in opinion or attitudes • Association with key brand attributes	• Visit website • Attend the event • Buy the product • Play the game/contest • Download coupon
Earned	• Organic search rank • Message inclusion • Impressions • Net positive impressions	• Readership • Message recall & retention • Awareness • Call center calls • URL visits	• Purchase consideration • Change in opinion or attitudes • Association with key brand attributes	• Visit the store • Attend the event • Buy the product • Vote for/against • Make a donation
Shared	• Opportunities to see • Branded mentions • Share of positive online discussion • Comment sentiment • Number of Followers, Likers	• Comments/Post Ratio • Number of links • Number of RTs • Follower RT % • Bookmarks/votes/likes • Resolution Rate • Number of @ mentions • Subscribers	• Tell a friend • Likelihood to recommend to a friend • Ratings • Reviews	• Visit the store • Attend the event • Buy the product • Vote for/against • Make a donation • Visit the website • Redeem coupon
Owned	• Unique visitors, cost per unique visitor • Page views • Click-thrus • Search rank	• Return visits • Interaction rate • Re-commenters • Duration (time spent) • Subscriptions	• Tell a friend • Change in opinions or attitudes • Association with key brand attributes	• Download white paper • Download game or app • Buy the product • Request more info • Conversions

So, for each of your campaigns, in advance of executing any work, think about how what you are trying to achieve will fit into a similar framework. And before you rush out to spend money on the latest all-singing and all-dancing automated platform, ask yourself whether this will really be giving you the insight and measurement that you need. As always, ask yourself what success would look like, and then think which would be the appropriate metrics to demonstrate this.

The last word should go to Amber Naslund, who co-authored with Jay Baer the recent must-read book *The Now Revolution*. In a post entitled The Most Powerful Social Media Measurement Tool Money Can Buy,[162] Amber says:

> 'With so many pieces of information floating around, we are more pressed than ever to find something, anything that can help us make sense of the mess. Tools and apps and platforms abound, smashing together data with alacrity, and pouring out more data as a response.
>
> Measurement has become almost as bad of a battle cry as 'influence' or 'awareness' or 'Community'. We have millions of pieces of information out there, and if we can come up with any way of distilling them into something that feels simple, we cry eureka! and slather it all over our reports like it tells us everything we want to know.
>
> But software and tools and automated rankings and everything of the stripe leaves one feature off the list, the feature that only that Human 1.0 can bring to you: Critical Thinking.
>
> The ability to look at a number and ask hmmm, where did that come from? Is that accurate? Complete? Relevant? Does it matter? Why does it matter, and what other information do I need to pair it with in order to make it matter? What is this number actually telling me, and can I improve upon it by changing how we gather it somehow?
>
> Only the human brain is capable of accurately and consistently critiquing and evaluating some of the most important qualitative things around data: context, nuance, sarcasm, unspoken implication, the dynamics of the ecosystem that sprouted the numbers, the impact that the gathering mechanism has on the numbers, understanding what

---

[162]Brass Tack Thinking, The Most Powerful Social Media Measurement Tool Money Can Buy: http://cipr.co/xxIfKk

other numbers and data should be related to one in order to make it potentially meaningful.'

Amber's advice makes perfect sense. No amount of numbers, scores and indexes are going to tell you whether you are achieving your specific objectives. That takes some thought, a tailored approach and human brain power.

Richard Bagnall MCIPR (@richardbagnall) ran Metrica for 15 years, during which time the company grew to become one of the world's largest PR measurement consultancies. Having integrated the business with Durrants and Gorkana, he is now a board director of Gorkana Group. Richard chairs AMEC's Social Media Measurement Standards Group.

Part VI

Skills

Chapter 20

Daljit Bhurji

The PR consultant of today faces a communications landscape almost unrecognisable compared to that of 20 years ago. While both veterans and novices need to develop and maintain a new and evolving toolkit, the rise of social media has made some of the fundamental skills of the PR profession more valuable than ever.

The list of special abilities that the modern PR superhero is expected to possess grows ever longer. Visit Google and it's not difficult to find blog posts listing the Top 20 or so 'essential' skills required to be successful in PR. Today, you apparently need to be a master of HTML coding, easily film and edit a hit viral video, develop a (basic) Facebook app, intimately understand the editorial agenda of the FT, feel at ease discussing marketing ROI with a CEO and then, after lunch . . . if you happen to be this mythical individual, please do send me your YouTube CV, we're always hiring!

Like those features in glossy magazines on how to be the best possible lover, back in the real world, these 'skill lists' can trigger self-induced anxiety and demotivation in the pursuit of an impossible PR perfection. It is not my intention to add to the worry already felt by many senior professionals who understand the risks of not staying relevant. Or to the thousands of graduates desperate to impress and get their first PR career break. The perfect PR professional does not exist. Whether it's in-house or in-agency, it really is impossible for one individual to excel at every discipline required of the 21st century practitioner.

This is why multidisciplinary teams (whether in-house or in-agency) will be the future of the communications industry. Developing individual skill sets will be as important as ever, but their worth will be greatly diminished if they are housed in a silo, rather than integrated across the marcomms landscape.

So what does the 'ideal' PR professional entering the second decade of a new century look like? Well, like the proverbial snowflake, no two are the same, but I think there is a commonality of structure which makes them instantly recognisable. It's what I call the Y-Shaped PR Professional, with breadth and depth across three broad areas of expertise: storytelling, content and technology platforms. Covering everything that falls under these headings would obviously be beyond the scope of a single book, let alone a single chapter, so what follows is a focus on a few of the key characteristics.

1. The storyteller

Let's start with modern storytelling. Across all areas of PR, we work in organisations – or are hired by them – to create and share brand stories. We look at a client's business and communication objectives and create story-driven campaigns that connect with audiences in order to promote understanding, manage perceptions and change behaviour. While the reach and third-party endorsement that traditional media offer remain immensely powerful, the rise of social media has also effectively turned every organisation into a media company.

Brands now have the capability to use digital channels to listen and speak to mass audiences directly and facilitate customer-to-customer conversations. The era of one-way brand storytelling is over; getting your audiences to co-create your story is the future. The rise of social media has made the craft of storytelling more valuable than ever, which is why it needs to form the sturdy trunk of the Y-Shaped PR Professional.

Key to developing your storytelling skills is a deep knowledge of the subject matter. As a foundation, we need to invest time in understanding our clients' businesses, wider industry and, above all, customers, inside out. However, in the social media world there is little room for corporate fairy tales – transparency triumphs. As audiences are able to give a real-time verdict and check facts almost instantly, so stories need to gel with the experiences that consumers have had with the brand and be open about the evidence we use to back them up.

However, PR practitioners face growing competition when it comes to exerting influence over that storytelling role.

Integrated storytelling

As the mass of PR awards won by Tourism Queensland's 'Best job in the world' campaign shows, a great PR idea today is just as likely to come from an advertising or media agency. Against an evolving media backdrop, the neat little niches that different types of agency used to occupy are blurring. A new generation of marketing and communication directors is rising through the ranks and, for most of them, the best big campaign idea wins, regardless of where it comes from. And, increasingly, the ideas which clients regard as the best are those that can integrate across multiple marketing channels, rather than those which sit in just one silo.

For PR professionals to compete in this environment requires a change in storytelling mindset and skill set. We need to ask ourselves some key questions: will this idea work beyond just editorial coverage, or beyond just a Facebook Fan Page? What is the campaign amplification role that PR can play? How do we make the campaign whole bigger than the sum of its parts? To answer these questions effectively requires much broader and deeper knowledge of the marketing mix beyond PR. We need to invest more time in understanding advertising, media, search and digital disciplines and agencies, including how they fight for their share of the marketing budget and how they measure their success. On that last point there is much the PR industry can learn from our friends in advertising.

The PR professionals that will compete best in the future will be those who look beyond just the pages of *PR Week* to understand the wider marketing landscape around them. As we increasingly work as part of multi-agency and multidisciplinary teams, clients will prize individuals who understand integrated storytelling. This more collaborative and competitive way of working will also bring those softer skills of tenacity and diplomacy to the fore, as brands demand that everyone plays together nicely.

2. The content creator

The next branch of the Y-Shaped PR Professional is the content creator. Once we have our brand stories, what will be the best ways to bring them to life, have them shared and allow audiences to shape how they develop? While I will come on to the rising importance of multimedia content to PR, we should avoid believing all the hype about the 'end of copy' in marketing. It would be more than slightly naïve to dismiss what has been one of our primary forms of communication since the 4th millennium BC.

Whether it's a 1000-word opinion piece, a Facebook comment or a 140-character Tweet, the ability to write well remains a core PR skill. As someone who has been reading PR job application forms from graduates for the past ten years, individuals with solid writing skills are becoming increasingly rare. From a recruiter's standpoint it remains the first thing we look for and notice. Social media have arguably elevated the importance of writing skills even further!

As any journalist will tell you, writing for *The Sun* is technically much more difficult than writing for *The Sunday Times*. Short-form writing, whether a blog post or Tweet, demands brevity. It also usually requires the ability to convey wit and empathy and reflect a specific brand voice and personality. These are not basic writing skills and even for those with a strong writing base, honing this ability demands training and practice.

In a crowded digital world the ability to find and share written content also demands that content is written with an understanding of search engine optimisation. What are the keywords and phrases that your target audience will be typing into Google? Sparkling copy in isolation is no longer enough. Luckily, Google's free Keyword Tool is perfect for leading you through this process.

Visual content

In the social media world, the old adage that a picture speaks a thousand words has never been so true. Large amounts of text need to be used in the right marketing situation, not in every situation.

The way in which many people consume media online and across multiple devices and platforms means that attention spans are shrinking. As we graze the Web, bite-size pieces of information, whether photos, videos or infographics, which can be consumed quickly and shared easily, are in demand.

Creating visual content is not something which can be done for free, but it does not always require a big investment of budget either. Where necessary, we need to work with designers and video producers, but we should also think more deeply about how to re-purpose the vast amount of content that organisations produce every year. Could an edited version of a presentation be given a new lease of life via SlideShare? Could the CEO's foreword to the annual company report also be delivered as a three-minute video, with you behind the camcorder?

Content curation

PR professionals, whether in-house or in-agency, are also being given responsibility for building and managing social media communities for organisations, particularly on Facebook and Twitter. Content curation and management has emerged as a skill set with growing importance. But perhaps this shouldn't come as too much of a surprise given PR's heritage in being able to speak to different audiences, display diplomacy and understand the difference between mountains and molehills. Ultimately it's about earning attention and engagement through being interesting – a core part of PR's genetic makeup.

I particularly like the analogy of a great community manager behaving like the perfect party host, who makes sure that there are the right mix of people, introduces guests to one another and throws in the odd game to get those who are a bit shy involved. It is about being part of the conversation while not constantly demanding to be the centre of attention. Implementing community management effectively requires complete immersion in a community; it is not something you can dip in and out of, so do ensure you have the time to do the job properly.

3. Technology enthusiasts

In the modern PR landscape, an effective storytelling and content strategy is impossible without a thorough understanding of the technology platforms that power social media. This is the final crucial plank of the Y-Shaped PR Professional. Now, don't panic. This doesn't mean we all need to rush out and get a degree in IT to continue working in PR, but it does mean investing time in using and understanding key online platforms. In that delightful American phrase we 'need to eat our own dog food' when it comes to social media.

While your traditional PR skills have been hidden behind closed doors, your social media expertise is much more public, with limited distinction between your online personal and professional personas. It's therefore important to consider how much of your experimentation with different social media sites you want to do under the radar and which platforms you will invest in to form part of your personal brand. From a professional perspective, Twitter in particular has become indispensable even for the most traditional of PR people, as more and more journalists use the service as part of the story-pitching process.

Real-time tools

First-hand experience of social media sites remains the best way to learn, but the PR person's technology toolkit now needs to extend beyond MS Office and media databases. The 24-hour news cycle has not quite been reduced to 24 seconds, but social media have further increased the pace of PR. Luckily, technology tools have been developed to help PR people to track and respond to the real-time nature of social media. Social media monitoring tools like Radian6 have the ability to track impacts on online reputation with third-party tools like TweetDeck and Conversocial making it easier to sort, view and post updates across multiple social media feeds and channels.

Social media have increased the time pressures that exist in an already stressful industry.

Mastering these types of tools and services requires a time investment up front that improves ongoing efficiency. The always-on nature of PR has elevated that core PR skill of time management to a whole new level, but technology can be the PR person's best friend in making it through the day.

Data and analytics

As well as mastering the 'front end' of social media tools and applications, it has become even more important for PR professionals to understand the powerful data and analytics that lie underneath. Google has made a huge impact on the PR industry and one of its greatest contributions has been Google Analytics. This free tool, which is intuitive enough for the ordinary user, has given brands and their agencies easy access to a wider range of insights on online consumer behaviour. Other social media platforms have followed Google's lead, with the likes of Facebook Insights putting hugely valuable information into the hands of PR professionals.

The fact that PR is becoming more data driven is a positive step-change for the industry and advanced skills in data manipulation and modelling will become invaluable as 'media planning' becomes more central to campaign design and evaluation. Those rare beasts that join the PR profession from a scientific or engineering background may have a natural advantage in this data-rich environment, but we should never lose sight of the consumers who lie behind the numbers.

Insatiable curiosity, insatiable scepticism

Having the right attitude is just as important as possessing hard PR skills. The pace of change within digital can be bewildering, and we all need to devote more time to stay on top of industry news and developments. Luckily, finding this news and seeing what is significant is another benefit of being embedded within, and active on, social networks with industry peers. However, enthusiasm and interest for social media need to be tempered by a sceptical and questioning mind.

One of the greatest criticisms of the digital PR industry is that it is too easily distracted by the latest 'shiny technical object.' This can add to the digital confusion felt by clients and distract them from the priority of delivering effective and measurable results. The extreme hype in January 2011 following the launch of Q&A site Quora is a prime example of the potentially distorting effect of the social media echo chamber. The intensity of the online chatter even led to trade magazines rushing out double-page features asking if Quora was the new Twitter, and pondering what the impact on mainstream brands would be. A year on, those who were a little more cautious have been vindicated and the answers to those questions have proved to be 'No' and 'Next to nothing'.

Blindly following the digital herd is not a sign of being digitally 'with it'. On the contrary, jumping on the latest bandwagon is a recognisable trait of self-titled 'social media gurus'. Experiment and play around, share new discoveries, but ask those fundamental questions about demographics, reach and longevity before raving to clients about the next social media channel they need to start budgeting for.

The pace of change for communicators in the next decade is unlikely to slacken, which may give some of the specifics of this chapter a particularly short shelf-life. However, looking at the key areas of storytelling, content and technology platforms should prove a more enduring framework for assessing the gaps in your own capabilities and evaluating the talents of colleagues and potential new recruits. Continuous professional development will be more important than ever, but we also need to be careful not to confuse knowledge, skills and expertise.

Keeping on top of trends and expanding knowledge across as many areas of PR and social media as possible should be our goal, but the skills we choose to develop need to be more specific to our strengths. The jack of all trades, but master of none will have limited value in the future. We all need to look at our areas of interest and current expertise and develop our own unique set of PR superpowers for the future!

Daljit Bhurji (@daljit_bhurji) is managing director of Diffusion, an integrated PR agency helping to drive social media campaigns for clients including Mothercare, Air New Zealand, CNN, The Conservatives and L'Oreal. As well as his CIPR work, Daljit also sits on the IAB Social Media Council, helping to develop policy and industry standards for the UK's digital marketing sector.

Chapter 21

THE FUTURE OF PR EDUCATION

Richard Bailey

This chapter considers the role of education in the development of public relations professionalism and explores the potential and the problems posed by the emergence of social media and the current uncertain political and economic environment.

Is public relations a relatively simple craft that anyone with sufficient common sense and experience can practise? Or is it a complex managerial activity that requires lifelong learning?

These questions are not easy to answer definitively because both positions are true. For most of the 20th century, amateurs dominated the field – and some of these are still in senior positions and educating today's students.

Many celebrated practitioners are proud of their lack of qualifications. 'I fell into publicity because I failed to get into university to read history,' writes Mark Borkowski.[163] Lord Chadlington, who founded what became the world's biggest PR consultancy, is reported as saying, 'When I started out in public relations, it was a business that people went into because they weren't good at anything else . . . I thought that I'd like to start my own business. And as I wasn't very good at anything, I decided I'd better start a PR firm.'[164] Lynne Franks is another well-known practitioner whose business career does not appear to have been harmed by a lack of formal education.

---

[163] Mark Borkowski, *The Fame Formula*, Sidgwick and Jackson, 2008, ISBN 978-0283070396.
[164] Lord Chadlington cited in Morris and Goldsworthy, *PR – A Persuasive Industry?*, Palgrave Macmillan, ISBN 978-0230205840.

Their experiences are typical of the 20th century – the first century of public relations. But these examples do not prove a point. History is written by the winners and the example of a few outliers in the past does not indicate the future. John Major may have become prime minister without a university degree, but he stands alone among recent occupants of 10 Downing Street. David Cameron's First Class degree in Politics, Philosophy and Economics from Oxford University is more typical. Cameron also worked in a public relations role before becoming an MP.

Public relations developed as a practice before it developed as an academic or professional discipline. Public relations degree courses in the UK are little more than two decades old, and the CIPR's professional qualifications only began in the late 1990s. So we are only beginning to see the emergence of PR graduates and those with professional PR qualifications into the most senior management positions.

The question here is not about the usefulness or otherwise of a PR degree, but of the value of education to public relations. While on-the-job experience may still be sufficient for learning the craft of public relations, managing a public relations function and reporting to senior executives requires well-developed analytical skills and a good understanding of the context and limitations of the role, and mastery of suitable management and evaluation methods.

What's wrong with public relations?

The authors of the influential *Cluetrain Manifesto* (www.cluetrain.com)[165] were merciless in their analysis of PR's credibility problem. 'Everyone – including many PR people – senses that something is deeply phony about the profession. And it's not hard to see what it is. Take the standard computer-industry press release. With few exceptions, it describes an "announcement" that was not made, for a product that was not available, quoting people who never said anything, for distribution to a list of people who mostly consider it trash.'[166]

---

[165]*The Cluetrain Manifesto*: http://cipr.co/w6oILi

[166]Rick Levine *et al*, *The Cluetrain Manifesto*: tenth anniversary edition, Basic Books, ISBN 978-0465018659.

The same authors suggest how the situation could be improved. 'The best of the people in PR are not PR types at all. They understand they aren't censors, they're the company's best conversationalists. Their job – their craft – is to discern stories the market actually wants to hear, to help journalists write stories that tell the truth, to bring people into conversation rather than protect them from it . . . In the age of the Web where hype blows up in your face and spin gets taken as an insult, the real work of PR will be more important than ever.'[167]

The Cluetrain Manifesto was written before the emergence of social media, and it frames the PR role as media relations – but this suggestion of PR's growing importance as 'the company's best conversationalists' is intriguing. Its analysis that PR is becoming more important than ever is supported by other influential voices; Sir Martin Sorrell runs WPP, the world's largest marketing services group. He gave a talk in 2008 describing the 'remarkable renaissance of public relations'. First among the six reasons he gave for this remarkable renaissance was social media: 'a natural territory for public relations'.[168]

So, while public relations may have become discredited in the public imagination and in the view of many journalists, it is seen as a growing force by marketing specialists and is a valued service in public, private and third sector organisations.

Marketers are not slow to recognise the power of public relations. When the Cannes Lions advertising industry awards created a new category for public relations, the first winner (in 2009) was the celebrated 'best job in the world' campaign for Queensland Tourism.

This memorable campaign created a dream role of island caretaker on the Great Barrier Reef, perfectly timed for the Northern Hemisphere winter, and solicited video applications from those wanting to give this up for a dream job with a large salary. The winner, a British man, had few duties other than to write blog posts about his experiences. The result was a brilliant viral

---

[167]Ibid. 164.
[168]Martin Sorrell, Public Relations: The Story Behind a Remarkable Renaissance: http://cipr.co/y2kKcv

campaign across traditional and social media and more than a year's 'free' publicity for Queensland in Australia.

The campaign is a good example of how public relations can be used to get people talking, without the huge expense of a global advertising campaign. But there's one problem with this narrative: the winning team behind the campaign was Brisbane-based advertising agency, Nitro (now SapientNitro).

It is possible for public relations to emerge strongly from the shadows of advertising (it's ten years since Al Ries and Laura Ries wrote the provocatively-titled book *The Fall of Advertising and the Rise of PR*), but also for public relations practitioners to be usurped by a new breed of marketing or communications consultant skilled at selecting the right message for the appropriate media regardless of marketing discipline.

So how can practitioners prepare to seize the opportunities presented by the disruption of social media and the changing political and economic environment?

Education and professionalism

We have professional bodies with their codes of conduct, we have professional qualifications, we even have a royal charter – but public relations does not command professional status in the same way as, say, medicine or the law. It is not necessary to have gained these qualifications, nor even to be a member of a professional body, to practise.

Public relations is closer in status to management than to the full professions. MBAs have existed for decades as a managerial qualification, but it's not necessary to gain one before setting up a private business, nor even before running a public enterprise.

Management consultancy is the closest equivalent to public relations. It's not a 'closed shop' profession, though its entry requirements are high in terms of the intellect and energies of practitioners, and the important role of education and training is evident in such a challenging and competitive business service. New recruits have a range of degree qualifications and prior work experience.

The obvious difference between public relations and management consultancy is that the majority of PR roles are 'in-house' whereas almost all management consultants work for external consultancies.

The role of education and training is evidently important for consultancies, as it's a means of competitive advantage since the skills, knowledge and talents of consultants are vital in a service business that only sells know-how.

But what about in-house practitioners? Education and training should be even more important here, as most in-house practitioners work in small teams, so there is less opportunity to learn from experienced peers and gain fresh new insights.

Open source learning and recruitment

Two anecdotes should illustrate how open education is becoming. A year or so ago I was speaking to the European head of one of the world's largest PR consultancy networks and mentioned in passing the name of one of our graduates whom his firm had recently hired in its London office. 'Ah, yes,' he said, mentioning the graduate's name, 'we'd been tracking him for some time.'

The old world of qualification–advertisement–application is becoming replaced by a more fluid world in which individual students and practitioners manage their own reputations online and connections can be made at any time between recruiters and job seekers. It is even possible to imagine a world where a graduate's online influence (as assessed by tools such as Klout and PeerIndex) might be more important than their degree classification. This is why I've been running a 'social student' ranking of PR students on social media at Behind the Spin (www.behindthespin.com).[169]

The second anecdote relates to school students choosing universities. Last year, I noticed an ambitious A-level student posting responses to some of our first-year university assignments on her blog. She was in the process of applying to university, waiting for offers and hoping to gain the expected A-level results, yet she was doing more than preparing for university. She was participating in assignments, discussing the course and the university with current

---

[169] *Behind the Spin*: http://cipr.co/KpdfEt

students and making herself known to the lecturing team. In the process, she was cementing her decision over her preferred course and university.

Many educators resist such openness – and often for good reason. It may damage a student's reputation (and that of the course and university) for sub-standard assignments to appear online. It makes more work for lecturers if they are expected to develop relationships with students who are not yet on the course. Some institutions prefer to keep teaching materials behind the firewall of a Virtual Learning Environment rather than make use of open learning tools such as blogs and wikis – though MIT[170] has been a pioneer for the past ten years in making its teaching material and assignments publicly available through its OpenCourseWare and MITx[171] initiatives.

The challenge for educational institutions is to recognise that they are operating in a competitive environment and to develop appropriate public relations strategies designed to enhance reputation and recruitment. It is likely that this will involve opening the doors of universities (metaphorically and literally) to outsiders.

It is possible to imagine a range of provision from more intense two-year degree programmes through to much longer part-time and distance learning provision attracting those with work and family commitments. Funding changes will force many universities to become more like the Open University.

But universities do not hold a monopoly on public relations education. The CIPR Diploma, a professional qualification, is currently taught by several universities. It is also offered by private training companies – through face-to-face delivery and in an online version.

Enabling lifelong learning

The professional project requires a shift towards lifelong learning, with the CIPR promoting its Accredited Practitioner[172] and Chartered Practitioner[173] continuous professional development schemes.

---

[170]MIT: http://cipr.co/yitTtB

[171]MIT News, What is MITx?: http://cipr.co/xMeUDX

[172]CIPR, Accredited Practitioner: http://cipr.co/accred-practitioner

[173]CIPR, Chartered Practitioner: http://cipr.co/chartered-practitioner

At present, there is a false separation between education and practice, learning and doing. This is wasteful and inefficient and it leads to some absurdities. For example, any student of public relations should be able to mount a reasoned critique of Advertising Value Equivalency (AVE) as a valid measure of public relations activity. This isn't just academic squeamishness – AVEs were condemned by industry body AMEC in the Barcelona Principles[174] of 2010.

Yet the same students and graduates often return to the workplace from their studies and cheerfully do as expected by continuing to present a monthly analysis of the value of PR assessed by AVE.

This is an example of the compartmentalisation of education as belonging in the classroom, and having limited impact on what goes on in the office.

Much more can and should be done by academics, practitioners and publishers to break down the walls of their silos. Here's my wish list of actions that could help to foster a culture of lifelong learning in public relations:

- Trade newspaper *PR Week* should report on the large education and training sector and should copy from professional journals in featuring reviews of new books and research of relevance to practitioners.
- Continuous professional development (CPD) should be built in to the process of renewing individual membership of the CIPR and PRCA. So each member, at renewal, should be asked to report on what they did in the past year to develop their skills and knowledge – and what they did to give something back to society or their community.
- Academics and academic publishers should be encouraged to break out of their closed circles and make their work more accessible to practitioners and students. This partly refers to the business model of academic publishers, and partly to the communication skills of research academics.
- Universities should start competing in an open educational market, recognising their many assets (libraries, the English language, the global status of UK public relations, teaching and research expertise). Courses should be available in attractive formats to everyone from school leavers to the retired.

---

[174]CIPR, Barcelona Principles: http://cipr.co/barcelona-principles

At the start of this chapter I asked two questions: is public relations a relatively simple craft that anyone with sufficient common sense and experience can practise? Or is it a complex managerial activity that requires lifelong learning?

There is a continued role for craft skills in public relations. In addition to the traditional skills (writing, presenting, media handling) the social media age requires practitioners to have some familiarity with online publishing and measurement tools.

But the real challenge for practitioners is to help organisations navigate the many problems and paradoxes they face – and to ensure their continued legitimacy in the face of the conflicting expectations of shareholders, employees, trades unions, politicians and the wider society. As Morris and Goldsworthy write in their new textbook,[175] 'PR people are among the few people in an organisation – the others are the chief executive and the financial director – who are involved in almost everything of significance that happens to it.'

Public relations will continue to grow in size and significance – and this brings added responsibility and challenge to those in senior PR positions. We need to encourage a culture of lifelong learning to ensure that practitioners are well placed to seize the many opportunities presented to them.

Richard Bailey MCIPR (@behindthespin) is a senior lecturer in public relations at Leeds Metropolitan University, where he is course leader for CIPR professional courses. He also tutors for PR Academy and leads a course in Public Relations and Public Affairs from a European Perspective for Johns Hopkins University.

---

[175]Trevor Morris and Simon Goldsworthy, *PR Today: The Authoritative Guide to Public Relations,* Palgrave Macmillan, 2011, ISBN 978-0230240094.

Part VII

Industry Change

Chapter 22

EMPLOYEE ENGAGEMENT: HOW SOCIAL MEDIA ARE CHANGING INTERNAL COMMUNICATION

Rachel Miller

With the advent of social media making their way into the workplace, this chapter considers how they are changing internal communication and enhancing employee engagement.

In the words of the late, great Steve Jobs, 'You've got to start with the customer experience and work back toward the technology – not the other way around.'

From a professional communicator's point of view, you've got to start with the communication and work back towards the technology, be that social media or traditional methods like face-to-face. Questions you may ask yourself are:

- What am I trying to achieve?
- Who is my audience?
- What do I want people to think, feel or do differently as a result of my communication?
- What action or behaviour am I driving?
- What's my message?
- How will the conversation start?
- How can it be two-way?

- What tools and channels will I use?
- How will I capture feedback?
- What will I measure?

Note that the channel/tool you will use is towards the end of that list. The focus is on the input and action you're driving. Once you know the answer to the preceding questions, channel choice becomes easier. Simply choosing a channel to be 'seen' to use it will not work if you're not clear as to why it's the best choice for your culture and organisation. More on this later.

The title of this chapter is Employee engagement: how social media are changing internal communication. Are they changing it? I think so. Employee expectations have certainly changed over the past few years as people wish to communicate in their professional lives in the same way that they communicate in their personal lives.

Expectations have shifted, so employees expect more – more speed, more transparency across organisations and from senior leadership, more information and the ability to comment immediately.

It's not good enough to have to wait until the next publication of the monthly magazine. Employees expect to be able to have their say and share their views in real time, in the same way they do at home. This is where I think social media are changing internal communication and employee engagement.

Steve Jobs also said, 'You can't just ask customers what they want and then try to give that to them. By the time you get it built, they'll want something new.' I think that quote sums up internal communications perfectly. In essence, once you've gathered your focus group feedback and employee survey opinions, produced an action plan and rolled out something new, employees are thinking ahead to the next aspect of communication and their expectations have shifted again.

In the same way, it's not enough for communications professionals to simply know the difference between the various social networking tools and techniques on the market; you need to be able to demonstrate how organisations can use social media to improve day-to-day business.

Top tip

Grow your network, read about best practice, meet with other comms professionals and seek to understand how social media are implemented in reality. What works? What doesn't? There are so many conferences highlighting these case studies at the moment. If you can't attend, check out internal comms blogs afterwards to ensure you have the opportunity to keep updated on this constantly evolving area. I've started to report[176] on such events via my blog, Diary of an internal communicator, and am encouraging other comms professionals to do the same, as time and budget do not allow everyone to attend everything.

Measurement

Social media can and should be measured. This was highlighted by the International Association for the Measurement and Evaluation of Communication (AMEC) as part of the Barcelona Principles, which were supported by CIPR amongst others. Your focus should be on measuring media results (outputs) in order to demonstrate effectiveness. You can read more about the Barcelona Principles online.[177]

Social media and employee engagement

I think social media can enhance employee engagement in many ways by:

- opening up new feedback channels;
- encouraging collaboration across silos;

---

[176]Diary of an internal communicator, Rachel Miller, Been anywhere good lately? 29 October 2011: http://cipr.co/z95SnO
[177]CIPR, Barcelona Principles: http://cipr.co/barcelona-principles

- horizontal networking by breaking down hierarchies;
- being all encompassing and interactive;
- their approachability, as employees pick and choose what and who to engage with.

All of these benefits are fantastic to be able to demonstrate within any organisation, and social media have a role to play in making this happen. Social networking sites not only work well within companies but also externally, as they can be used for recruitment, communication, connection and engagement.

It's all about being social

Do you know the difference between social communication and social media? The key word in those terms – social – is the path to success.

Setting aside all the gadgets, theories and noise that are around, if you peel back the layers to the core, social communication and, simpler than that, the effectiveness of using word of mouth to deliver change and communicate with those around you, is at the heart of the matter.

In his book *From Lincoln to LinkedIn*, Mike Klein says that, 'Through using social communication techniques and tools, you have access to an approach to communication that channels power, precision and passion directly to the challenges you and your organisation face.'

I agree with Klein's thinking, which says that, at its core, social communication is built around tribes and networks that are constantly forming and reforming around organisations. He encourages professional communicators to step back and think about the informal social and conversational networks that drive real communication, not just the tools that may help give it shape and velocity. You can read more about his book in my blog.[178]

In my view, social media and social communication offer communications professionals the opportunity to use different media to reach your

---

[178]Diary of an internal communicator, Rachel Miller, Why social media has Tweet all to do with new technology, 23 May 2011: http://cipr.co/xPzyVU

audience and create two-way conversations. It is important to determine what you are trying to achieve before introducing any new channel, be that a briefing system or a wiki, to ensure you are choosing the right tool for the job.

Simply introducing a whizzy social media site because it is the latest 'must-have' is a recipe for disaster if you're not clear why it is right for the organisation and its culture. It's always worth taking calculated risks and trying something new, but do listen to your employees and ensure you're matching business needs with your internal communication recommendations.

If you're introducing something new, is it time to retire an existing channel? Be brave and make decisions that are right for your organisation – sometimes a channel has come to the end of its useful life if your company has changed the way it communicates. If this is the case, be bold about what you lose and what you use. Pilot new things, dip a toe in the water, but, equally importantly, get employees involved in the process and decision making.

Top tip

Don't view social media as something that are done 'to' employees, but 'for' and 'with' them.

Top tip

Don't always use the 'c word' – communication. Talk the language of business, particularly when looking at social media.

How to use social media

Research by Melcrum into 'How to use social media to solve critical internal communication issues' sets out to identify the biggest benefit for internal communicators who have put together a business case for the use of social media within their organisations. The top three replies were:

1. Innovation and idea exchange (41.5%).
2. Employee engagement (38.4%).
3. Knowledge management and collaboration (30.8%).

This was backed up by the fact that 54.3% of the respondents said that 'getting employees to talk, share information and collaborate' was the 'most effective' use of social media within global organisations. Building communities was second, and connecting to and learning from Generation Y employees was the third most effective use of social media.

I think this research helps underline the benefits of social media's role in internal communication, particularly when solving issues, and wonder whether productivity would feature in the results if this survey was repeated in a couple of years' time.

So, you have got your business case lined up, but what about the financial side? What benefits can you prove for employee engagement?

Employee engagement and the bottom line

According to some researchers and practitioners, there is a strong link between effective internal communications and superior company performance.[179]

Extensive research has also been carried out over the years on how boosting employee engagement affects the bottom line of organisations. In March 2011, the *Financial Times* featured research by Gallup which showed that

---

[179]Trahant, B. (2008) Six secrets of top-performing organizations, *Public Manager*, 37(3), 68–75; Kitchen, P.J. and Daly, F. (2002) Internal communication during change management, *Corporate Communications: An International Journal*, 7(1), 46–53.

improving staff engagement could provide serious financial returns. Gallup estimated that disengagement in the US cost more than $300 billion (£186 billion) every year in lost productivity alone, and in 2008 it estimated the cost to the British economy was between £59.4 billion and £64.7 billion.

In the same year, a report by the UK Institute of Employment Studies found that increasing investment in engagement by 10% generated an extra £1500 of profit per employee annually.

So we know that employee engagement is important, and we know that social media can enhance internal communication, but the missing link is how.

Looking at the principles of successful change implementation by Kotter,[180] the fundamental steps are:

1. Establishing a sense of urgency.
2. Forming a powerful group to lead the change.
3. Creating a vision about the change and communicating it widely.
4. Empowering others to act on the vision.
5. Planning for and creating short-term wins.
6. Consolidating improvements.

In my view, these principles apply to initiating social media to aid internal communication and employee engagement within organisations. If you follow these principles it will create a comprehensive, cohesive approach, taking into account the rapidly changing world of communications and the expectations mentioned at the start of this chapter.

Bill Quirke[181] takes it one step further when talking about principles for change implementation including maximising the sense of continuity and stability, being proactive, anticipating rumours and explaining the implications for the individual. Adding this to your approach will start you off in the right way. I'd also add listening into the mix – asking your target audience to share their views at every step.

---

[180]Kotter, J.P. (1996) *Leading Change*, Harvard Business School Press.
[181]Quirke, B. (2008) *Making the Connections: Using Internal Communication to Turn Strategy into Action*, Gower Publishing.

> # Top tip
>
> Approach the introduction of social media as you would any other change project.

There is still a level of scepticism about social media and their use within the workplace. This is particularly prevalent from board level executives. My advice is to gather your allies and to keep on learning.

Gather your allies

Work with IT to ask their advice before recommending a channel. In the same way comms professionals don't like it when people say 'we need a newsletter' without realising their problem is engagement, and face-to-face would help, IT professionals don't like it when their comms colleagues approach them with all the answers. Work together with your business partners to identify what is possible within your organisation, based on your understanding of communication and culture and their understanding of technical possibilities.

Keep on learning

Internal communicators have many opportunities to increase their own understanding of employee engagement, internal communications and social media. Make sure you read what you can, attend courses where appropriate or even consider a professional qualification. You can find a list of resources on my blog.[182]

---

[182]Diary of an internal communicator, Rachel Miller, Rachel's resources: http://cipr.co/xeFUuX

Crystal ball gazing

What does the future look like for how social media will change internal communication?

As a fan of the *Back to the Future* films, I'd love to think there is a role for a hoverboard within communications – let's make it happen! But in all seriousness, the future of internal communication is being written now.

I think the future of social media and internal communication is that they will become so ingrained in the way we do business and communicate that we will stop using the phrase 'social media'. The focus will be on the connections, collaboration and communication – who's doing what, where they are doing it, what they think of it and how others can get involved.

Immediacy will continue to be key, with real-time communication an integral part of corporate communication, both internally and externally.

The lines between work, personal life and public persona will blur and people will be able to control who sees what as controls become more prevalent within social communication. These boundaries will become as natural as choosing whose number you put in your mobile, and will be very much business as usual.

Feedback and contributions from employees will ensure communicators can gauge reactions to content and tailor and adjust messaging and methods accordingly.

Chad Hurley, CEO of Delicious and co-founder of YouTube, is quoted as saying, 'Social media will be the main engine of discovery, giving us the ability to find the signal within the noise. As people's networks and interactions expand, massive data sets will generate predictive models that will know what you want before you look for it.'

I recently came across a clip on YouTube[183] showing how a one-year-old thought a magazine was a broken iPad because she couldn't work out why the pages wouldn't react to her pinching them. It's not a question of age, as technology touches everyone's ability to communicate, but as younger generations enter the workplace, will internal communications methods meet their requirements?

---

[183]YouTube, Baby Thinks a Magazine is a Broken iPad: http://cipr.co/zhyV9h

I mentioned the shift in expectations that we are seeing in workplaces now. What can we expect in the future? I think more of the same. We will see remote working becoming more popular as technology means people don't need to physically be in the same building to feel connected and engaged with their peers and managers across the globe. The role of internal communicators is to ensure the right channels are in place to enable communication to happen.

Social media are here to stay. Back in 1876, an infamous Western Union internal memo had this to say about the telephone, 'This "telephone" has too many shortcomings to be seriously considered as a means of communication. This device is inherently of no value to use.'

In the same way, I believe the social media doubters will be forced to recognise that this collaborative way of sharing knowledge, creating understanding and relationships and communicating is as crucial for businesses as an effective IT or payroll system.

Top tip

If you are privileged enough to work in corporate communications, do ask your experts, your employees, for their views about social media. Make smart decisions based on your own expert understanding of internal communications and the opinions of those around you.

Enjoy the journey.

Rachel Miller (@AllthingsIC) started her career as a journalist and has worked agency side and in-house for companies including BSkyB, L'Oréal, Visa, Tube Lines and London Overground. Named in *PR Week*'s Top 29 under 29, she's a Kingston Internal Communications Management postgraduate, mentors comms professionals and blogs at www.rachmiller.com.

Chapter 23

Mark Pack

There is much hype about how developments in technology and the internet are changing communications. However, change is not inevitable and the lessons are not all so new.

Not everyone has modernised

Imagine yourself in (or, if you are old enough, remember back to) the world of 40 years ago. Back then the government ran two intermittent advertising campaigns that I want you to think about – one against smoking and one in favour of voting.

Both those advertising campaigns have evolved over the years. Anti-smoking campaigns have attracted some of the best advertising talent, with a range of memorable, shocking, award-winning advertisements, garnering such accolades as a gold award at the Institute of Practitioners in Advertising (IPA) effectiveness awards.

The very quality of the adverts and the size of their budgets have shown up the limitations of the advertising medium, which is why current anti-smoking efforts are massively different from the old days. Behavioural economics, nudge theories, social media, societal norms – all are now part of a much more diverse and sophisticated approach than the old one of 'stick out an advert'.

Now think about the voting advertisements. The need for them has become greater over the last 40 years as turnout has fallen. Despite this, such campaigns, most recently under the wing of the Electoral Commission, are still deeply traditional in their approach. Read through the Electoral Commission's evaluation reports of their campaigns in recent years and you get the best of the industry in terms of the approach to thorough evaluation. However, you also get a highly old-fashioned, narrow approach to influencing behaviour that is where the anti-smoking efforts were 40 years ago but most certainly are not any more.

Understanding why there is that difference is the key to understanding the future development of public sector communications and the role of social media.

Why tradition hangs on

One reason is quite simple: the sort of sophisticated analysis and action that is now part of anti-smoking work is much harder to do than designing a good advertisement. Anti-smoking efforts have – quite rightly – been a magnet for smart minds, cutting-edge techniques and significant budgets. Being modern is very hard both at the technical and managerial levels. Bringing change and innovation to an organisation is not easy. As Machiavelli himself put it, 'There is nothing more difficult to take in hand, more perilous to conduct, or more uncertain in its success, than to take the lead in the introduction of a new order of things.'

Moreover, it is not simply the case that, as new approaches become less new, everyone gets good at them and they can be widely used. There are many very well-established approaches, around for decades, which still are used badly across huge swathes of the public (or indeed private) sector.

Direct mail at its best is a highly advanced skill, with large amounts of accumulated knowledge and decades of experience to call on. Yet look at the latest letter reminding you about a hospital appointment and the chances are it is of a quality that would get a marketing intern politely shown the door.

This problem bedevils efforts to raise turnout – just take a look at the design of the poll card, the one piece of direct mail sent by electoral authorities to every voter at election time. The designs are not simply old fashioned. The abuse of fonts, the failure to prioritise information and the design for the convenience of administration rather than communication means they were never good.

A second reason is that in anti-smoking work pretty much no one has to worry about its impact on different tobacco brands. Being generally against smoking is OK, and if that happens to damage one firm more than another, so be it. Yet turnout at elections is very different. If efforts help one party, that inevitably means it is at the expense of others, and far from generating a 'so be it' shrug of the shoulders, it provokes controversy.

As a result, efforts to promote turnout at elections are still very broad brush. There is a limited amount of targeting which is seen as generally acceptable, such as particular ethnic communities, but the idea of singling out intermittent voters on council estates, for example, immediately runs into those allegations of partisanship. Yet can you imagine an anti-smoking campaign which did not specifically seek out smokers? Tellingly, where there has been targeted work, it has come from either politicians or pressure groups, both of whom are, in their own ways, less restricted by concerns over impartiality between candidates and parties.

The third reason is that for those interested in health, smoking has been seen as a major issue, whilst for those involved in administering elections, turnout has been seen as an incidental issue (if indeed it has been seen as an issue for them to be concerned about at all).

Transport for London: both old and new

This trio of explanations shows how there are underlying factors which explain the patchy spread of the most modern approaches. There is more to the story than simply department X is good or profession Y is bad. As a result, even within one organisation you can see both the modern and the traditional, with some areas up to date and others lagging behind. A good example of this is the body responsible for public transport in London, Transport for London (TfL).

In some respects, TfL has modernised its communications in extremely impressive ways. Walk up to a bus stop today and you will see a whole raft of communication changes designed to encourage people to use buses more. The Tube-like bus route maps, the timing indicators, the maps of the area and so on. Transport for London has called on worldwide experience of what and how to communicate in order to encourage more use of public transport (including, ironically, learning some useful lessons from Sydney, where, to a British eye, the bus stops now look like a return to the 1970s, so undeveloped are they).

Yet in other respects, Transport for London mirrors not the anti-smoking improvements but the election turnout traditions and worse. Take the simple question of asking people to walk on the correct side of corridors or stairs. With increasing numbers often making these pinch points in the transport infrastructure, funnelling people into the right places is not a matter of bossiness or convenience; it is often essential to keeping the service working.

However, take a look at Transport for London's approach to this and you get taken into a world where the hope is that old-fashioned adverts and typography can win out. Put the sign in red. Add in some capital letters. Make the sign bigger. It is the old-fashioned approach to communication as SHOUT-ING. If it does not work, shout louder. Perhaps with added exclamation marks.

What we do not see from Transport for London is the equivalent of the anti-smoking campaigning sophistication. The longer-term efforts to change social norms, the redesigns to instinctively funnel people towards, rather than away from, the desired behaviour or the word-of-mouth campaigns to spread the message.

Why this contrast? That we see both behaviours in the same organisation makes the point that there are more subtle factors at work simply than whether an organisation is good or modern. Transport for London has both modern and old-fashioned faces because some areas have been given priority – with the best minds, the most time and the budgets – whilst others have been neglected. As with the contrast between anti-smoking and pro-voting campaigns, the patchiness is caused by being modern being hard, and by some issues being seen as important and deserving attention and others not. (The question of how many people use public transport and why gets frequent study and attention, for example from the London Assembly's Transport Committee; the congestion and reduced capacity from people in the 'wrong' places does not.)

What the dual nature of Transport for London's approach illustrates, as does the smoking/voting contrast, is that there is no simple inevitability that every area of public sector communications will change across the board.

A state of flux

Moreover, where there is change, it is not necessarily simply about technology or the rise of social media, but rather about traditional issues being enhanced and expanded to new areas by technology. For example, in Australia the publication of best-selling healthy diet advice books, produced by Australia's national science agency CSIRO, has been an effective way of getting useful and accurate health information into the hands of people, pushing to one side and down the bestseller charts recipe collections with less healthy options and advice with questionable scientific roots.

In the UK the NHS has taken an online-savvy approach to the same question of getting good information in front of people rather than bad, with its emphasis on search engine optimisation work, so people searching for information about symptoms online, for example, are more likely to find reliable information from the NHS's experts rather than dodgy information from a firm selling an unproven 'treatment'.

Although book publishing is centuries old, while search engine optimisation is relatively new, the principle in both cases is the same – make your own good quality information readily and conveniently available so that it is what gets used by people rather than lower quality information from others.

Yet where the NHS's search efforts have been only cautious is where there is also great scope for further innovation in both communication and the supply of services – using the public as co-creators and co-providers. In the simple NHS search case, what has not really been tapped is the wider concerned public community, who, through appropriate blog posts, added links and shares on social networks, could further boost the NHS's search engine presence. Instead, the public has been left uninvolved and indeed the question of the degree to which public involvement should be welcome has been one of the issues at the heart of the Patient Opinion/NHS Choices debates over the relative merits of having patient reviews of parts of the NHS on unofficial sites, official sites or not at all.

Seeing the public as allies and co-communicators rather than a passive audience to be communicated at requires a significant cultural shift which is only rarely present at the moment in the public sector. It is half-way towards a wider attempt to transform public services, with a shift from treating the public as passive consumers through to seeing them as active participants, in control and influencing others.

More digitally savvy approaches to communication are seeping out in areas that do not face quite the same obstacles, such as the government's social media friendly anti-cyberbullying campaign, which has been raising the profile of the issue and knowledge of when and where to turn for help. It has, though, not been alone in the field, with Google's own work on the same problem often over-shadowing that from the government and illustrating how, in the complex world of many communicators, it is no longer simply a case of the public sector having the field to itself to shout loudly at everyone.

Lessons from the Romans

So what does the future hold? It is not the promise of a whole new world, for the tale of communication and technology is that innovation only rarely kills off the old in its entirety. We still speak. We still write. We still publish books. Neither the eons nor the centuries of progress since any of those were first done have killed them off.

Even some of the newer features of social media are not really that new, for it was the Romans who had the Acta Diurna.

The Acta Diurna were daily public notices, posted up in public locations around Rome. Rich people would send scribes to find the latest Acta Diurna, make a copy and bring it to them. Provincial governors, too, would keep in touch with the news by having copies made and dispatched to them. Caesar did not go round threatening to feed people to the lions for breaking his copyright. There are four lessons from this which still apply:

- *Lesson one* – put your information where the audience is. The Acta Diurna were put up where the public was, taking the news to them.
- *Lesson two* – spice up information with interesting human colour. (Or, in the 21st century, a photo of a cat.[184] Though Pliny the Elder did recount a story he read in them about a dog that faithfully followed his dead master's body into the river at the funeral.)
- *Lesson three* – make it easy for people to share your information and it will spread far. Cicero himself commented on how widely the Acta Diurna spread, even if not always accurately: 'I receive letters from princes of foreign states thanking me for the part I have taken in making them kings, while I did not even know that there were such persons in the world'.
- *Lesson four* – if you want to influence what people think about you, do not leave it to others to do all the communication. By being a popular source of news, the Acta Diurna were also an effective form of news management.

Or, in other words – when someone tries to dazzle you with the wondrous newness or fiendish technicalities of a communications medium, remember that the basic principles remain much the same.

Dr Mark Pack is Head of Digital for MHP Communications, one of the UK's ten largest communications consultancies. He ran the Liberal Democrats' 2001 and 2005 internet general election campaigns and has worked with both the public and private sectors in online communications. This is the 21st book he has contributed to as an editor or author.

---

[184]ROFLCAT, 'I'm in ur newspaper writin mah colum': http://cipr.co/ACzesG

Chapter 24

MODERNISING PUBLIC AFFAIRS FOR THE DIGITAL AGE

Stuart Bruce

The enormous growth of the social Web means that many companies have embraced it as part of their marketing communications activity. Far fewer have recognised the threats and embraced the opportunities it provides for corporate relations and public affairs.

> 'It is difficult, indeed dangerous, to underestimate the huge changes this revolution will bring or the power of developing technologies to build and destroy not just companies, but whole countries.'

When Rupert Murdoch said these words in March 2006, he didn't know the eventual role social media would play in the Arab Spring, but he thought that somewhere, sometime, it would bring countries and companies down. However, it is doubtful that he envisaged its role in the demise of his own company's best-selling tabloid newspaper the *News of the World*.

Public affairs is changing

The 2010 general election was billed by many as the UK's first 'social media' election. Many of the same people were as quick to jump to the post-election conclusion that it hadn't happened. But after the frothy commentary died down, there has been some hard academic analysis which clearly shows that the internet and social media were a significant, but not decisive, factor.

Political parties and even government itself have embraced social media. So what does this mean for public affairs professionals? It means the old world of private networking and briefings is slowly, but resolutely, disappearing. Even when you want to keep something quiet, the plethora of blogs, social networks, user-generated content and citizen journalists all make it far more likely to become public anyway. In a world where lobbying has such a disreputable reputation, greater transparency can only be a good thing. By conducting more activity in public, it is far less likely that anything else will leak out unexpectedly.

Two of the most compelling reasons for integrating social media into public affairs practice are that firstly it is where people spend their time. Internet users now spend more time on social networks than they do on mainstream media sites such as the BBC. Secondly, social media are a primary source of information for policy makers, journalists and other influencers. With both of these reasons, search plays an essential role, as it is one of the primary ways people find information.

But before we can examine the role of social media within public affairs, we must first define what we mean by public affairs, as it is far more than just lobbying. Broadly speaking, public affairs falls into five spheres of activity:

- intelligence gathering, monitoring and analysis;
- policy development;
- relationships and engagement with policy makers and influencers;
- message development and dissemination;
- issues management.

Using social media for public affairs practice

Social media impact on each of these spheres in a variety of interdependent ways.

One of the most fundamental parts of most public affairs activity is stakeholder mapping to identify potential allies and opposition. Social media provide you with a means of researching who these potential allies and opponents might be, often at a far greater depth than traditional ways of doing so. Not only can you identify the organisations and institutions – such as special interest groups and think tanks – that are relevant, but you can also drill down into the individuals within those organisations. Using LinkedIn, Twitter and Facebook, you can find out more about not only their professional lives and interests, but also more about their personal interests and backgrounds.

Monitoring and analysing conversations on social media and social networks can also provide a valuable insight into public opinion on public policy issues. Monitoring conversations on specialist online forums, Facebook and LinkedIn groups can help improve understanding of what the most involved stakeholders are saying and thinking. This monitoring of issues and trends can also act as a valuable early warning radar to pick up signs that an issue is moving up the public policy agenda because activists and other stakeholders are talking about it more and using more emotive language.

As well as simply monitoring conversations, it is also possible to participate in conversations and start new ones in order to improve policy making. Often, when a particular issue reaches the stage of potential legislation or regulation it is too late to have a major say as the broad parameters are already set. By participating at a much earlier stage when the issue is still being discussed and debated by stakeholders in special interest groups and think tanks, it can be possible to help frame the discussion around that policy.

Content is influence

More than 80% of internet sessions start with search – be it internet wide on search engines like Google or Bing, or on the search functions of individual websites such as Facebook, YouTube or Twitter.

It is therefore more than likely that those you are seeking to influence will, at some time, use internet search to find out more about the issue or policy you want to manage or influence. That means when you invest time and resources in creating policy briefing papers, research reports, news releases and question and answer documents, you want to maximise their effectiveness online. This means optimising all of the content for search and making it easier for people to share and use it, or elements of it, on their own social profiles and websites. By ensuring that your content on a particular policy issue ranks highly on organic internet search, you can actually start to frame the debate around the policy at the very outset.

As well as optimising content for organic search, it is also possible to very cost effectively use paid internet advertising. Because the keywords you are interested in are often very niche, the cost per click or impression can be very low. During the 2010 election, the Conservative Party used pay per click advertising very effectively by buying Google AdWords for keywords based on that day's news to drive people to its campaign website. It is also possible to buy advertising on Facebook and LinkedIn which can be targeted to very specific demographics in terms of age, gender, geography, etc.

A more public affairs specific advertising option is MessageSpace, which provides advertising on the major political blogs and websites in the UK. MessageSpace advertising can be targeted by IP address, so it is possible to have different adverts appear depending on the network the computer is on. For example, a campaign could be set up so that one advert appeared on computers in Conservative Central Office and another on computers in the Treasury Department.

Content management systems such as WordPress make it very fast and easy to set up individual sites to act as a hub for publishing the content. Depending on the objectives, this might be a site for a specific campaign or for a particular policy area or issue. If you use the right words as part of the website address (URL), it improves your search ranking for those keywords. The actual site itself might be a blog or a social media newsroom depending on the objectives and the stakeholders that need to be influenced. Publishing the content on multiple content and social platforms further increases its reach and improves its search ranking. Some of the most relevant platforms to use include YouTube or Vimeo for video, SlideShare for PowerPoint (repurpose briefing papers into a slide deck), Flickr or Picassa for photos and Scribd or Edocr for document sharing.

Many public affairs campaigns put great store in securing favourable traditional media coverage to draw attention and gain support. Frequently, far less effort is put in to working with social media. However, a blog like *Order Order* by Guido Fawkes has a far greater readership than *The Spectator*, *New Statesman* and *The House Magazine* combined. Similarly, 43% of news sharing is via social media, making it a powerful channel for increasing the reach and influence of the campaign.

Engagement and relationships

The most frequent objection about social media and social networks from senior public affairs practitioners is that personal face-to-face relationships are vital to effective public policy work. And they are right, but what social media and networks can do is to broaden the circle of stakeholders engaged with, and strengthen those relationships. Jimmy Leach, when he was head of digital diplomacy at the Foreign and Commonwealth Office, pointed out that one of the reasons for the importance of using social channels is that, 'Even if you think you know everyone you need to, you need to listen and talk to more people than you think.'

What social media and social networks enable is a better understanding about those you're seeking relationships with and more frequent engagement than would be possible via traditional means. Interacting with think tank researchers, politicians, special advisers and other stakeholders can be done far more frequently and easily on Twitter, Facebook and LinkedIn than it can in an offline environment where you can just have infrequent meetings and phone calls.

Social media, especially Twitter, are also a powerful means of engaging with journalists, especially those with political beats. Many political news stories now break on Twitter before they are reported on mainstream news outlets. Twitter can also be used to direct significant traffic to a website or other online resource that you might have created for your policy agenda.

The tone of voice that is used for online engagement is very important. Adopting a too-formal or corporate jargon-laden approach is unlikely to succeed and indeed is more likely to have a negative effect. It is important to make your approach conversational and personal, but also remember that different tones are required for different networks. For example, for most people, Facebook is a very personal space that they use for interacting with friends. Twitter is more frequently more of a mix between the personal and the professional.

Social media and social networks also enable you to find or create communities of interest and engage with them on an ongoing basis far more easily than many traditional channels. It is important when measuring and analysing social media activity that the right metrics and targets are used. An audience of 150–200 people for a video webcast on a public policy issue is an excellent result if you compare it to holding a traditional meeting or seminar. That would be a good size audience. But too frequently, people compare it to audiences for a viral video on YouTube and deem it a failure.

Another rapidly spreading form of technology making a major impact on engagement is the smartphone. In today's fast-paced news cycle there is an engaged audience to speeches that will be able to check facts and claims as they are delivered and challenge them on Twitter, where you can rebut them just as quickly, even while the speech is still being delivered. It is possible to lose control of your messages and the news agenda before your speaker even comes off stage.

Issues management

Often, organisations only recognise the importance of social media when they are forced to in order to respond to an issue or crisis. The reaction of many corporations and organisations under attack on social media and social networks is to be defensive and bring in the lawyers to attempt to stifle criticism. This can have its place, but it is rare. 'Keep your friends close, keep your enemies closer' was the wise counsel of Sun Tzu, Machiavelli and Don Corleone. It can apply equally to online critics.

The result of sending legal letters to vociferous online critics will often be that they simply publish the documents to highlight the bullying approach being adopted to prevent what they see as free speech. If you're trying to get material removed from the site, the result is frequently that it does disappear from there only to spring up again on hundreds or thousands of other social profiles and sites across the internet.

Organisations and companies that already have an established presence within the social Web will already have identified relevant stakeholders and developed relationships with them. This early and ongoing engagement puts them in a far more favourable position when an issue does arise and can help prevent it turning into a crisis, as there is already a favourable reputation and store of goodwill.

New strategies for a new era

The result of all these changes is that companies and organisations need to adopt new strategies to take account of the changed political, social and news environments. The old model of public affairs was 'push', where you had a policy issue that needed to be addressed so you identified your stakeholders and pushed your messages and policy agenda out to them in the hope of influencing them to achieve change. The new model of public affairs is symmetrical, where not only are you pushing out your messages but you're also pulling stakeholders in by creating compelling reasons for them to engage with you and your policy agenda.

The effect of all this content creation and engagement is ultimately to help you achieve your public policy objectives. Digital public affairs doesn't replace or sit separately to traditional activity, but should be at the core of your public affairs strategy. Digital public affairs acts as an accelerant, increasing the effectiveness of traditional activity. It makes identifying and influencing influencers faster, easier and more powerful. It makes it faster and easier to broaden and strengthen support from interested and supportive stakeholders.

As the social Web becomes ever-more pervasive, it will be incumbent upon professional public affairs practitioners to integrate it into their strategies and everyday activities.

Stuart Bruce MCIPR (@stuartbruce) has worked in PR and public affairs for more than 20 years and, in 2003, started one of the world's first PR blogs. His experience includes counselling global companies like Sony Ericsson, Unilever, PayPal and GSK as well as the United Nations, UK and overseas government departments, the Labour Party and senior UK cabinet ministers.

Chapter 25

Simon Collister

As our lives become increasingly oriented around online networks, the third sector is realising that the social Web offers opportunities for communicating with and mobilising supporters. This new, networked reality is also giving rise to new forms of campaigning organisation.

There is an undeniable transformation that is taking place in the world around us. It is a transformation that the sociologist Manuel Castell terms 'The Rise of The Network Society'. It translates as a shift from an ordered, hierarchical world to one where 'networks constitute the new social morphology of our societies and the diffusion of networking logic substantially modifies the operations and outcomes in processes of production, experience, power and culture.'

Thus, networks structure the way we live and their impact extends all the way from how organisations operate internally and connect with other institutions right through to the way they communicate with the public and campaign for social change.

This chapter aims to demonstrate how social forces underpinning the recent rise of online networks and social media are hard-wired into the third sector's ethos. As a result, community and voluntary organisations are in a strong position to embrace social media and maximise the potential it offers as a communications and campaigning infrastructure.

From this empowered starting point, case studies illustrate how non-profit organisations can – and do – overcome reticence towards new technologies to take advantage of the social Web. At the same time, it will also provide a pragmatic analysis of some of the challenges the sector faces in a rapidly shifting and evolving media landscape.

Before we can fully grasp the impact and opportunities of this transformation, we need to go right back to the origins of the modern-day third sector.

From the early mutual organisations of the 19th century through to the progressive social movements of the 1960s, the third sector has built itself around groups of people sharing similar values, with a passion to deliver a solution to social problems where it didn't exist before.

These same values and drivers are arguably exactly the same ones that have built the social Web and power social media. As a result, the third sector is perhaps best placed to make the most of the new communications landscape.

As a future-watching report by the National Council for Voluntary Organisations – *ICT Foresight: How Online Communities Can Make the Internet Work for the Voluntary and Community Sector* – put it back in 2007, 'If the late nineteenth century was the golden age of mutual institutions, clubs and societies, the early twenty-first century is a new golden age of networks.'

Although this 'new golden age' carries with it many benefits to community and voluntary organisations, it also brings with it a number of challenges as the scale and rapid growth of the social Web open up new possibilities for social change which anyone with an internet connection can tap into.

If we look more closely at the specific forces driving this new networked reality for third sector organisations, we can distil two key factors: firstly, social capital (motivation based on non-financial rewards experienced through using social cooperation to achieve shared goals) and secondly, self-organisation (networks being created by self-organised groups using free and low-cost technology).

Intrinsically the social Web engenders the creation and distribution of social capital on a scale never seen before. The volunteerism and shared goodwill from which civil society and the third sector grew has become a central platform in mainstream society.

The emergence of low-cost, Web-based tools which make up the infrastructure of social media is connecting individuals with shared values and shared goals at an unprecedented rate and on a global scale. This means that people with shared values can easily find similarly minded people wherever they live, plan action for social change and work together to achieve it.

For example, in a non-networked world, establishing, funding and managing a successful global non-profit organisation raising more than $500,000 would require significant foresight, funds and resources. Now, anyone can use social media like blogs, Twitter or Facebook to find like-minded people who share the same world view and desire for social change. Then, they can turn to online fundraising tools such as Kickstarter or JustGiving to raise money to turn their shared vision into reality. And finally, by spreading the coordination of this new networked non-profit across its many members around the globe, large and cumbersome tasks are broken down into granular actions that can be completed quickly and efficiently through the organisation's distributed infrastructure.

This may sound too idealistic to be true, but it's a condensed account of how Twestival sprang from a group of friends on Twitter to a global movement that raised $1.75 million for good causes in four years.

What Twestival brings to life is the reality that third sector organisations, according to the NCVO's ICT Foresight report, are 'increasingly being bypassed and power is shifting away from top-down hierarchies and towards more fluid and participative networks.'

Operating in the new networked reality

While this grassroots innovation is immensely powerful and desirable for civil society, it also risks posing a series of significant challenges to traditional civil society organisations.

Social media require organisations to fundamentally reorient communications and campaigning as an activity that is brought to life through finding and engaging in conversations happening across relevant social networks, just as Twestival did. Rather than simply broadcasting to supporters or potential donors through newsletters, advertising or traditional PR, you now need to engage and tell people about your cause and mobilise them to take action.

This transformation represents the transition best captured by social change consultant and blogger, David Wilcox, as one from an institutional – or 'Join Us' – organisation to a networked – or 'Join In' – organisation.

Fully networked 'Join In' non-profits operate as just another node within social media-enabled networks. They recognise that there are other active individuals and even other organisations whose world-views and goals are potentially aligned.

While the emergence of global, self-organised advocacy networks may pose specific threats to the third sector, these networks offer established non-profit organisations significant opportunities to extend their reach and improve their effectiveness.

So what do non-profit organisations need to do to make the most of operating in the new networked reality?

First and foremost, traditional non-profit organisations need to identify and start listening to wider online networks and communities that are self-organised around an issue or topic strategically aligned with their own goals.

For example, the international development charity, ActionAid, has recently developed and implemented a real-time campaign-tracking tool that enables the organisation to identify and analyse online networks discussing key policy or campaign issues.

Using a monitoring dashboard to evaluate conversations and actions empowers ActionAid to adapt its communication and fundraising strategies based on up-to-the-minute evidence of how key topics are being publicly received, talked about and shared through online networks.

This use of information and insight generated empowers traditional non-profits to make the most of self-organised online networks: by analysing and understanding what motivates the like-minded individuals creating and consuming social media, traditional non-profits can plan social media campaigns that are strategically aligned with existing and powerful communities.

This enables traditional organisations to extend their reach to wider, highly networked and active audiences, meaning campaigns can go further and achieve greater levels of mobilisation.

Oxfam has recognised the potential in gathering insights about online networks by reconfiguring its campaigns team to include a digital strategy planning and innovation role. The purpose of this role is to ensure that Oxfam's campaigns can tap into online advocates – both paid-up Oxfam members and others – learn from them, plan more effective campaigns and subsequently mobilise them in support of policy change.

Having planned a strategically aligned campaign, organisations then need to engage with online networks. The best way to achieve this is to remember that the ultimate goal is for the organisation to become another node in the network.

This requires two key attributes: firstly, be compatible and secondly, add value by contributing useful or relevant information. Organisations that fail to observe these points are less likely to succeed.

In practice, this means that as online networks have grown around free or low-cost and widely available technology, such as blogs, Facebook, Twitter and RSS, non-profit organisations should adopt these tools.

But social media are about more than technology. They are about building trusted relationships. As blogger and futurologist, Russell Davies, has observed, social media are 'a social thing; social norms apply'.

Non-profit organisations need to add useful and interesting content and conversation to social networks. Broadcasting information and not listening, or listening and talking but not putting back into the network are quick routes to failure.

The future is hybrid

If the 'listen, understand and engage' approach detailed above is an effective starting point to empower traditional 'Join Us' organisations to start shifting their social media activities towards the 'Join In' model, then perhaps the emergence of purely networked organisations like MoveOn.org, 38 Degrees and Avaaz offer us a glimpse of the future of non-profit and campaigning organisations empowered and super-charged by social media.

Director of Royal Holloway, University of London's New Political Communications Unit, Professor Andrew Chadwick, has identified a new breed of campaigning organisation which he believes represents 'new organisa-tional forms' that:

> 'exist only in hybrid form and could not function in the ways they do without the internet. These 'hybrid mobilisation movements' blend functions typically associated with political parties, interest groups, and social movements and switch between online and offline realms, and within and between campaigns.'

One of the most successful examples of this type of hybrid organisation is the UK-based campaigning platform, 38 Degrees. Named after 'the angle at which an avalanche happens', the 38 Degrees website declares that it is not a formal non-profit organisation, but rather 'a community of UK citizens who act together to create an avalanche for change. We work together in our hun-dreds of thousands to defend fairness, protect rights, promote peace, preserve the planet and deepen democracy.'

Although 38 Degrees has a small, core staff of hard-working campaign-ers, it believes that the 'real leadership of 38 Degrees comes from our members'. In fact, 38 Degrees members help decide upon which issues or causes the organisation campaigns; the community helps raise money to fund campaigns and the platform is now facilitating the offline mobilisation of self-organised groups geographically co-located.

This hybrid model has certainly paid off for 38 Degrees, with its members having helped achieve a number of campaign victories across a range of issues, including stopping the Coalition government's plans to sell off national forests; preventing the building of a US-style mega-dairy farm and halting plans by Donald Trump to evict families in Menie, Scotland in order to build a golf course.

While this type of networked campaigning favours newer, more agile organisations, there are still opportunities for older, more estab-lished third sector organisations to embrace social media and networks campaigning.

One example of the collision between these new social media-enabled 'hybrid' movements and traditional non-profit organisations is the Robin Hood Tax campaign.

The campaign, calling for the implementation of a Tobin Tax – a small tax on financial transactions to raise money to tackle global poverty – brings to life a clear single issue built by a coalition of leading NGOs and trade unions.

Recognising the clear benefits of campaigning as a single voice on a single platform, these organisations got together to create an umbrella campaign. Crucially they also recognised that the popularity of social media gave them the power to run a high-profile campaign at relatively low cost that engaged supporters from a range of different backgrounds and empowered them to take visible and measurable action. Robin Hood branded profiles have been created on leading social networks and a blog is used to share campaign news and updates while administration is provided from a virtual office with a skeleton staff co-opted from campaign partners.

As Anna Nolan, digital campaigner with the Robin Hood Tax (RHT) campaign, reveals, 'Once the campaign launched it became clear that people were keen to engage with the RHT coalition brand, and the place for those conversations became social media, particularly Facebook. Within a week of launch we had a community of 100,000 plus. From there we invested approximately 80% of digital capacity of the campaign to social media. This was not something we had planned to do but happened organically and we responded by shifting resources. On Facebook we established an active community based on the simple premise that when people talked to us we talked back. This became the space for debate, whilst we invested heavily, time wise, in conversation, an informal community of "ambassadors" was quickly established who soon took on the voice of RHT – they sign posted people to resources, encouraged actions and answered common FAQs. This meant little moderation was necessary by central coalition. Even now, more than 18 months after launch, over half of our Facebook Fans engage with us on at least a monthly basis.'

In essence, the Robin Hood Tax campaign created an inspiring single-issue campaign that used the power of networks to raise public opinion and mobilise support to the extent that the Tobin Tax is now a major issue on the G20's political agenda.

This was all achieved by leveraging support from the campaign's parent institutions while remaining agile enough to build, engage and empower a community of passionate advocates.

The picture being painted here is that the emergence of new, self-organised networks is a potent force for social change. It gives organisations the opportunity to build on the third sector's age-old ethos of harnessing passion and dedication to make the world a better, fairer place and connect with technologically-empowered networks of supporters and advocates to achieve even greater successes.

While the collision between traditional organisational models and the new networked reality for the third sector may throw up a few challenges along the way, the power of social media-enabled campaigning cannot be ignored.

As activist and academic, Dan McQuillan, puts it, 'the first law of Web 2.0 . . . says that people will do it anyway. Community groups and grassroots activists aren't waiting for large NGOs to decide whether social networks are kosher – they're just going ahead and using them.'

The third sector has a unique opportunity ahead of it and is historically in a strong position to make the most of the opportunities presented by social media. Thinking openly and honestly about the benefits social media brings; planning carefully and putting a road map in place will help organisations realise that another world is possible.

Simon Collister (@simoncollister) has worked in and consulted with the third sector for ten years. He is presently a senior lecturer in PR and social media at London College of Communications, University of the Arts London. Prior to that he was consultancy director with the leading social media agency, We Are Social. He has held digital positions with the PR firms Edelman and Weber Shandwick and is currently researching a PhD in power and networked media systems.

Part VIII

The Future

Chapter 26

Philip Sheldrake

The social Web has transformed PR practice massively, but information and communication technology innovations keep coming thick and fast. While we bed-in our response to the mass market's adoption of social media, and while we keep an eye on what's happening from week to week right now, it's time to take a look at what's just around the corner.

When George W. Bush was inaugurated for his second term in January 2005, no one uploaded a video to YouTube. When Italy beat France to win the 2006 FIFA World Cup final, fans didn't Tweet. Not once! No one in Europe mentioned it on Facebook. No one captured Fabio Grosso scoring the winner on an iPhone. No one jumped on Gmail to commiserate with French friends. No one used BlackBerry Messenger (BBM) to celebrate with Italian friends.

How things have changed in such a short time, but the revolution is far from complete. The evidence suggests that technology will advance faster this decade than the last, and so too, therefore, entrepreneurs' facility to wield it to our collective delight, confusion and amazement. I don't think it is too dramatic to say that we've only scratched the surface of this Web thing so far.

Every profession needs to keep abreast of the latest political, economic, social, technological, legal and environmental trends and adapt as needed. We've focused on some of the technology and social aspects in this book – Web and mobile-enabled social media.

And, as we have seen, our stakeholders' media habits, proclivities and expectations are changed massively from just a decade ago. The mechanisms by which influence goes around have shifted – and radically in some regards. Public relations practice has had to evolve with a fascinating mix of highs and lows, success and failure, as one might expect in such a fast-moving landscape full of unknown opportunities and hidden pitfalls.

Our frameworks for dealing with social media are maturing, and some of the UK's foremost experts have shared their knowledge with you here. But just in case you're feeling too comfortable, what better way to conclude the book than with a chapter taking a quick glimpse at the next chapter? After a book on so-called Web 2.0, I'm going to introduce you to so-called Web 3.0, and the 'Internet of Things'.

Three follows two

The first manifestation of the World Wide Web fundamentally connected documents with hyperlinks. It was the 'Web of documents', displayed as Web pages with a bit of e-commerce thrown in. We retrospectively labelled it Web 1.0, a name that came naturally once a conference documenting the emergence of social media was named Web 2.0.

I have seen 'Web 3.0' evoked in several different contexts, the most amusing effectively implying that Web 3.0 is Web 2.0 done really well! But no. Web 3.0 is the common name for a technology known as the Semantic Web.

Sir Tim Berners-Lee, the inventor of the World Wide Web, describes the Semantic Web as the Web becoming a universal medium for the exchange of data, information and knowledge. The Web itself 'understands' the meaning of all that Web 1.0 content and Web 2.0 social participation.

Just think about that for a minute.

Importantly, lest you think I reside in some kind of blue-sky hypothetical future, this transformation is happening around us right now. Amazon is doing it. Google loves it. Data.gov.uk lives it from the ground up. The BBC and Southampton University are global leaders, and a project known as dbpedia is translating Wikipedia into Semantic Web form.

In April 2010, the International Press Telecommunications Council announced the official launch and widespread adoption of its G2 family of news exchange standards supported by Agence France-Presse, Associated Press, dpa, The Press Association and Thomson Reuters. G2 contains some Web 3.0 components.

We have tried to divine meaning in the torrent of Web 2.0 contributions; the blog posts and comments, the tweets, +1s, Facebook updates and Likes, the product reviews, the YouTube and Flickr and forum chitter chatter. But capable social analytics remains the domain of those who can afford it, allowing them to, amongst other things, form an aggregate picture, more relative than absolute in its inferences and conclusions.

Now, with the advent of the Semantic Web, rather than just communicating in human readable formats, you're expected to communicate in Semantic Web ways. I say 'expected' simply because this way of communicating is coming of age and you probably wouldn't want to exclude yourself or your organisation from this way of communicating, in just the same way you've embraced all the forms of communication that have come before.

Perhaps, at the time this book goes to press, it's not too wide of the mark to say that Web 3.0 today is roughly where Web 1.0 was around 1996. Interestingly, the concept of search engine optimisation (SEO) entered modern lexicon in 1997. One wonders when public relations practitioners will begin to start optimising content for Semantic Web discovery.

Equally, *The Cluetrain Manifesto*[185] didn't set out the ramifications of the social Web for organisations until 1999. But while it's fairly early days yet for Web 3.0, think about the competitive advantage wrought by those early to Web 1.0.

I co-presented Web 3.0 with James Howard, Executive Product Manager, BBC Future Media, at the CIPR Social Media Conference 2011. As here, we felt it was a great way to finish proceedings, and I was able to introduce what I call 'machined' media.

You may be familiar with the 'paid, owned and earned' categorisation of media that emerged in 2009; well, we now have 'machined' media too[186] – content that is automatically discovered, presented and published by machines for humans.

---

[185]Wikipedia, *The Cluetrain Manifesto*: http://cipr.co/xUyirv

[186]Philip Sheldrake, The Influence View of Content – seeking something more useful than 'paid, owned, earned': http://cipr.co/AkWcZi

The reaction at the conference was best summarised in one tweet by the chair, Vikki Chowney:

> @Sheldrake introduces the concept of 'machined' media, heads explode around the room #ciprsm

While being a Web geek helps me grapple with such innovations, I can assure you my head hurts too! The Semantic Web is an exciting and fearsome vision and reality. And as if that wasn't enough . . .

Things

The phrase 'Internet of Things' refers to a network of objects not historically connected. We can consider four kinds of objects: the device containing electronics in order to fulfil its primary function (e.g. washing machines, air conditioning units and cars); the electrical device traditionally absent of sophisticated electronics (e.g. lighting, electric heaters and power distribution); non-electrical objects (e.g. food and drink packages, clothes and animals); and environmental sensors measuring variables (e.g. temperature, noise and moisture).

Just in case you were wondering how non-electrical items join the internet if they have no electrical power, I'm referring here to something called radio frequency identification (RFID). This technology is manifest with small tags that are physically attached to the item in question and hold digital information about the item that can be read remotely; as the item arrives at the warehouse for example, or as a cow is milked, or as a traveller uses her payment card on public transport, or her passport going through passport control, or as a book is checked in and out of a library.

I have seen estimates for the total number of items connected to the Internet of Things that vary from 16 billion in 2020 to more than 30 times that number. Either way, the 'things' will outnumber the approximately seven billion people on the planet by some margin.

But what on Earth has this got to do with public relations?

I had a go at synthesising a definition of PR during the PRSA's 'PR Defined' initiative towards the end of 2011:[187]

> 'The profession of public relations entails the planned and sustained effort to influence opinion and behaviour, and to be influenced similarly, in order to build mutual understanding and goodwill. This process is critical to maintaining and growing relevance, reputation and trust, and therefore public relations is central to setting and achieving organisational objectives.'

If we take as given that access to information may influence opinion and behaviour, and if information can be distilled from the data kicked off by the Internet of Things, then it stands to reason that the domain of public relations must include the Internet of Things.

How does the Internet of Things impact your market? How are your products transformed if you can continue to 'talk' to them during their useful lives? What new services spring up around this capability? How will you cater to the associated privacy ramifications? How will you integrate the information and knowledge distilled from your products in the field into your marketing communications? How might your public relations and customer service efforts need to blend?

Data, data, data

The Semantic Web and the Internet of Things give PR practitioners, and everyone else in the organisation come to that, and your publics, access to unprecedented and massive amounts of data; on top of Web 2.0 that is, and magnitudes more.

Whereas data paucity was the challenge of the 20th century, so-called 'big data' is both the challenge and opportunity of the 21st.

---

[187]Philip Sheldrake, Public Relations Defined – the anatomy of a candidate definition, ver 0.2: http://cipr.co/zLcv62

This book has been about navigating social media – understanding how to cope; forming a deeper appreciation as the basis for innovation. Now we must contemplate developing the skills of the PR professional to navigate this new ocean of data; indeed, to input into the design of your organisation's boat.

Philip Sheldrake (@sheldrake) is the author of *The Business of Influence: Reframing Marketing and PR for the Digital Age* (Wiley, 2011) and the Digital Marketing chapter of the CIM's book, *The Marketing Century*. He is a Chartered Engineer, Member of the CIPR, Founding Partner of Meanwhile, Founding Partner of Influence Crowd, Main Board Director of Intellect and Board Director of 6UK. He built and sold an award-winning PR consultancy. Philip co-founded the CIPR Social Media Panel and the CIPR Social Summer series; he chairs the CIPR's measurement and evaluation group and co-hosts CIPR TV. He blogs at philipsheldrake.com.

INDEX